DATE DUE

Brodart Co.   Cat. # 55 137 001   Printed in USA

AUSTRALIA
NEW ZEALAND
USA
VANCOUVER
WHISTLER
SQUAMISH
BLACKCOMB
ROUND HOUSE
MARK'S COWBOY MUSIC TENT
SLEIGH RIDE
THE VILLAGE
LOST LAKE
VILLAGE SQUATS
THE BOOT
MONS
PARKHURST
GREEN LAKE
SOO VALLEY
HWY 99

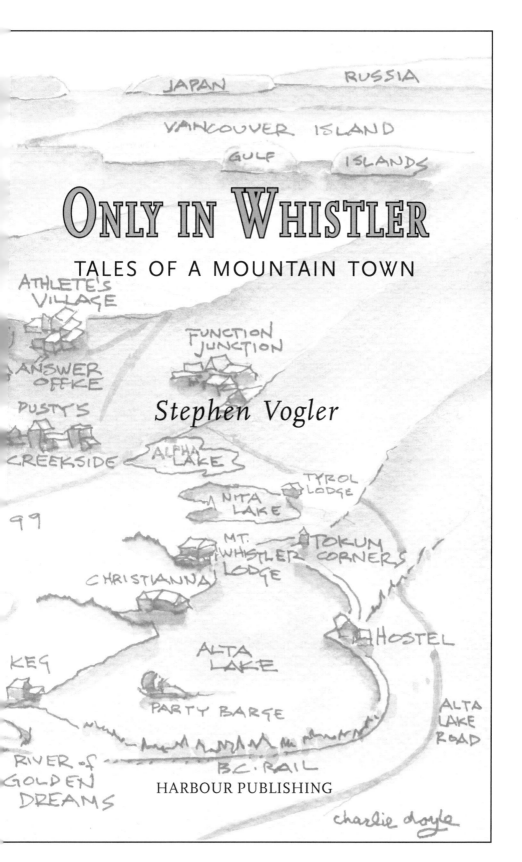

ONLY IN WHISTLER

TALES OF A MOUNTAIN TOWN

Stephen Vogler

HARBOUR PUBLISHING

JAPAN

RUSSIA

VANCOUVER ISLAND

GULF

ISLANDS

ATHLETE'S
VILLAGE

FUNCTION
JUNCTION

ANSWER
OFFICE

DUSTY'S

CREEKSIDE

ALPHA
LAKE

TYROL
LODGE

NITA
LAKE

99

MT.
WHISTLER
LODGE

TOKUM
CORNERS

CHRISTIANNA

ALTA
LAKE

HOSTEL

KEG

PARTY BARGE

ALTA
LAKE
ROAD

RIVER of
GOLDEN
DREAMS

BC RAIL

charlie doyle

Harbour Publishing Co. Ltd.
P.O. Box 219, Madeira Park, BC, V0N 2H0
www.harbourpublishing.com

Cover photograph by Gary McFarlane
Edited by Margaret Tessman
Map by Charlie Doyle
Cover design by Anna Comfort
Printed and bound in Canada

Harbour Publishing acknowl-
edges financial support from the
Government of Canada through
the Book Publishing Industry
Development Program and the
Canada Council for the Arts,
and from the Province of British
Columbia through the BC Arts
Council and the Book Publishing
Tax Credit.

Canada Council   Conseil des Arts
for the Arts   du Canada

BRITISH
COLUMBIA
ARTS COUNCIL
Supported by the Province of British Columbia

Library and Archives Canada Cataloguing in Publication

Vogler, Stephen, 1964–
Only in Whistler : tales of a mountain town / by Stephen Vogler.

Includes index.
ISBN 978-1-55017-504-2

1. Vogler, Stephen, 1964–. 2. Whistler (B.C.)—History. 3. Whistler
(B.C.)—Biography. I. Title.

FC3849.W44V63 2009   971.1'31   C2009-903547-2

To Peggy,

For support beyond measure

ACKNOWLEDGEMENTS

Thanks is due to many people who helped with the completion of this book. I am indebted to those who contributed to the lifeblood of the work by generously sharing their stories from Whistler and beyond. These include: Florence and Andy Petersen, Bonny and Andy Munster, Nigel Protter, Kashi and Bob Daniels, Shelley Phelan, Sue Ross, Catou Crookshank, Angela and Martin Mellor, Charlie Doyle, Mark Schnaidt, Brett Wood, Ian Bunbury, Tim Smith, Bob Colebrook, Peter Vogler, Robin Blechman, Pat Rowntree, Mark MacLaurin, Nigel Woods, Nancy Wilhelm-Morden, Derek Rhodes, Ace Mackay-Smith, Janine Jeffrey, Paul McNaught, Mike Walsh, Jen Jackson, Rob Hughes, Tammy Alain, Tanya Clark, Tim Staritt, Jordan White, Brian Walker, Stephanie Reesor, Eric Crowe, Roger Moxley, Steve Anderson, Jessica Hare Turner, Dave Kirk, Jim Watts, Karen and Dave Kay, and any others whose names I may have forgotten to include.

My penchant for telling the story and verifying the facts later was remedied by the excellent fact checking skills of Tim Smith. Others deserving of thanks in this department include Dave Steers, Shelley Phelan, Paul Bunbury, Kelly McGuire, Bob Barnett, Cliff Jennings, Bob Dawson, Jehanne Burns at Whistler Museum and Archives, the crew at Tapley's Pub and anyone else I may have questioned over the past year.

The list of people who contributed photographs is too large to include here but I'd especially like to thank Bonny Makarewicz, Toshi Kawano, Andy Dittrich, Greg Griffith, Brian Hydesmith, Chris Woodall, Dave Steers, Rod Harman, Colin Pitt-Taylor, Tim Smith and Charlie Doyle, as well as the dozens of people who dug through their photo albums in search of the elusive ice-skating shot. Thanks to my son Jonathan Vogler for his graphics skills in fixing an old photo, to Charlie Doyle for the original map and to Gary McFarlane for the cheeky cover image. The Ski Patrol Bomb Shack Museum previously appeared in a slightly altered form in *Mountain Life* magazine, Winter 2008.

It was a pleasure working with editor Margaret Tessman, Anna Comfort and Teresa Karbashewski in production, and with everyone else at Harbour Publishing. Finally, thanks to my family Peggy, Jonathan, Melissa and Katie for listening to the advance tellings of these stories at dinner over the past year.

CONTENTS

	Introduction	9
1	An Icy Stage	11
2	Squatters and Buses	21
3	On Dishwashing and Dead Horses	51
4	Hope You Like Jammin' Too	72
5	Up the Mountain	89
6	The Print Revolution	112
7	Working for a Living	148
8	The Ski Boot	174
9	Spring Thaw	201
10	Ullr, God of Skiing	225

Charlie Doyle, Gary "Chico" Autio and Rod McGowan emerge from their
squatters' cabins to climb Whistler's highest peak, Wedge Mountain, in 1979.
PHOTO TIM SMITH

Introduction

Whistler has been known as a ski destination for nearly half a century. Visitors are drawn from all over the world to its glacier-carved Coast Mountains, covered to the shoulder in temperate rain forest and blanketed by a healthy annual snowfall. There's something about sliding down mountains that mesmerizes us humans: the dance with gravity, the exhilaration, the connection to some deep cosmic force. Albert Einstein said he never felt so free as when he discovered that gravity is cancelled out by a falling body. Clearly he was a skier at heart.

But for all the allure of the mountains themselves, the lifeblood of a mountain town still pulsates strongest in the valley. Whistler's narrow, semi-confined geography holds an eclectic mix of souls who have climbed into its cradle-like shape and, for one reason or another, never left. We seek out the mountains for the thrill of adventure and to feel our connection to the universe and the gods, but it's in the valley where we create our collective experience. If the skier's or rider's tracks are his or her personal signature on the mountain, then the valley is the rich meeting place where those signatures intersect, in harmony and discord, tragedy and comedy.

I'm leery of the term "mountain culture," which is too often a mere recounting of mountain sports adventures. Having grown up in a family of fanatic skiers (fanatic enough to leave the city and move to a hippie ski-bum town of five hundred equally passionate souls in 1976), I got my fill of mountain sports competitions and pure dedication to the thrill of gravity in the earlier part of my life. I've since come to believe that going up the mountains is as much about earning the right to hunker down with friends at the end of the day as it is about fresh air and exercise.

The intense mountain experiences still occur on high, but culture is what happens in the valley, as it has since the dawn of humanity. It happens when we gather around the fire with a pint of beer (one of the major food groups in a ski town), a shot of whisky or a mug of tea, and recreate ourselves. We call it "après," from the French *après-ski*. As the stories emerge from the bartender, vacationer, waitress, ski jumper, go-go dancer, builder, artist and lawyer, we get glimpses of the true identity of this mountain town. Of course, the après sessions themselves sometimes spin out of control and generate a whole other layer of stories, as when we find ourselves in the nightclub at two in the morning with our ski boots still on.

The tales we tell are tall ones—a renegade barroom bronco, a propane-powered cappuccino machine, a three-legged hitchhiking dog—but the facts matter little compared to another kind of truth that emerges in their telling. We get to relive the experiences, enjoy a good laugh and discover how the stories of so many eccentric characters weave together into the fabric of a mountain town.

1

AN ICY STAGE

The year my family moved to Whistler was the worst
snow year ever. But in many ways 1976–77 was one of
Whistler's best years. At the heart of the valley, Alta Lake
froze thick enough to drive a '69 pickup truck across it and the
entire community, all five hundred locals and another thousand or so weekenders (turkeys or gorbies, as they were sometimes referred to then), congregated on the ice. There were ice-
hockey games and boot hockey for those without skates, figure
skating, ice sailing and *Eisstockschiessen* (a European version of
curling), and there were barbecues and beer kegs, parties and
romances, all happening out on the perfect sheet of ice that was
Alta Lake.

The winter had begun with typical snowfalls, but a Pineapple
Express in December washed away snow up to the 10,000-foot
level and was quickly followed by a lengthy cold snap. After
struggling through December, Whistler Mountain closed on
January 15 (it had hosted eight paying customers the previous

day) and the lake, with its free skating, continued to be the centre of life for the underemployed, the newly unemployed and anybody else who hadn't left for warmer climes. François Lepine, a local at the time, recounted his memories of that winter many years later in Whistler's *Pique Newsmagazine*: "Individuals who barely said hello to one another before became good friends playing hockey. Locals, who never skied on weekends, mixed with the weekenders on the ice for the first time. Older, established residents who only suffered the presence of ski bums as a necessary evil before—and certainly would never socialize with them—gained some respect for the ones that stuck it out and friendships across age groups developed that winter."

For a family new to the valley there was no better way to become acquainted with Whistler's cast of characters than to have the entire extended community arrayed on the icy stage of Alta Lake: ski bums, squatters, restaurateurs, liftees, mountain managers, kids, dogs and more dogs. With the town focus back on the lake, the lodges along the shore resumed their previous roles as social hubs of the community: Cosmic Fred held Sunday night movies at Mount Whistler Lodge; live bands played at the Christianna Inn; a warm fire could always be found at the Whistler Hostel; The Keg at Adventures West had dining and a thriving party scene. Even Rainbow Lodge was still standing, though it would be destroyed by fire the following spring, marking a true end to the Alta Lake era. The strange winter weather events of 1977 offered the lodges and the lake itself a kind of swan song before the huge changes sweeping into the valley hit with full force.

Just over a year before that unusual winter, the town of Alta Lake had been renamed and incorporated as the Resort Municipality of Whistler. The resort designation was a new experiment in local governance that would allow the municipality to meet the needs of local residents, absentee cabin or condominium owners (never referred to in the provincial Act of Parliament as turkeys or gorbies) and visitors to the resort. Whistler's first mayor and councillors were elected and appointed, a community plan was drawn up and plans for a centralized tourist village and another ski development on Blackcomb Mountain were launched.

Around the same time, my family embarked on its own experiment. We'd been skiing at Whistler every weekend and holiday for the past few years, and had started to visit more often in the summers as well. We stayed at the Tyrol Ski and Mountain Club, a modest but warm lodge in an idyllic setting beside Nita Lake that had begun to veer from its strictly Alpen European roots toward a broader demographic of members and visitors. As it happened, the caretaker position at the lodge was becoming available in the summer of 1976. Back in Richmond, where my brother and sister and I had grown

Hanging out in the backyard (Tyrol Rock) at the Tyrol Lodge with Whistler Mountain in the background. PHOTO COURTESY THE AUTHOR

up feasting on abandoned apple, pear and cherry orchards, the semi-rural lands were rapidly being paved over for a different kind of abundance: shopping malls and parking lots.

The clincher in our move to Whistler may have been the moment that our 1969 Oldsmobile Cutlass Supreme sailed off a cliff on the snowy highway just south of the Cheakamus Canyon in December 1975. A lone skinny tree stopped us from plunging to the canyon floor and we all emerged with minor injuries except for my dad, who left a row of teeth behind in the steering wheel. Perhaps this incident convinced my parents that rushing up to the mountains every Saturday morning could be hazardous to the family's health, and that moving to a ski-bum town of five hundred, where the de facto teen centre was the pinball machine at the 76 gas station, was a sound idea.

For a twelve-year-old passionately into skiing and reading books by Farley Mowat about the Canadian North, the idea of moving to a snowy mountain wilderness was paradise. The notion was far less appealing to my fourteen-year-old sister Vicky, who would be leaving behind her newly made high school friendships in Richmond in exchange for riding a school bus an hour to and from Pemberton each day. My sixteen-year-old brother Peter, though keen on the skiing, was equally unimpressed with the new high school arrangement. I was given a one-year reprieve from the lengthy bus ride as I entered grade seven at the newly built Myrtle Philip School beside the garbage dump that would soon be transformed into Whistler Village.

I shared a class, along with six other grade seven students at Myrtle Philip School, with the grade fives and sixes. My new friends and cohorts came from families who represented the full breadth of Whistler's social fabric. Compared with the typical two-parent families of 1970s Richmond, Whistler had its fair share of single moms and dads, and people generally embarking on new adventures in life. My friends lived in everything from hotel rooms and rental ski cabins to squatters' shacks and trailers. My living situation had its own oddities. The little two-bedroom caretaker's house at the Tyrol Lodge wasn't designed for a family of five with teenagers. To remedy the situation, my dad renovated a tiny old cabin next to the house into bedrooms for my brother and me. The cabin stood about twenty-five feet from the front door of the house, but the sometimes-snowy tramp to the bathroom was a fair trade-off for the independence it offered in my teenage years.

Matt Bolton became my new best friend that fall, and he showed me everything a local kid needed to know in our rapidly transforming town. While Al Raine was overseeing the engineering of the sewage treatment system and Whistler's mayor and councillors were visiting Victoria to convince the new Social Credit government that the Whistler experiment (hatched by the previous New Democrat government) was still a good idea, Matt and I were on the ground, in the trenches as it were, exploring the physical changes to the valley and testing the worthiness of the new infrastructure the way mischievous twelve- and thirteen-year-old boys are wont to do. Construction of the sewer line next to the railroad tracks along Nita Lake slowed the trains past the Tyrol Lodge to a crawl so that you could hop a freight the half-mile to Creekside. The little yellow speeder cars would also occasionally stop to give us rides. New power poles were being installed next to the sewer line and we collected the exotic blue glass insulators that hadn't been smashed when the old poles came down. When the workers had packed up for the day we investigated the Caterpillars, backhoes and drilling machines, the boxes of blasting caps and dynamite left lying around, and all the other implements necessary to lay a sewer pipe into the hard granite of a Coast Mountain valley.

Matt was a year older than me, and his dad, Jack, originally from Liverpool, had done some rock climbing in his day. He had one memorable story of a climbing friend who'd found a hiking boot at the bottom of a climb, foot still in it. In our forays around the valley, I recognized Matt's superior climbing abilities. It was clear that, good skier and athlete though I was, I hadn't developed that surefootedness on the rocks that only comes with living in the mountains. In short, I was still a flat-lander. Our dog Fanny, a relatively small St. Bernard, was going through similar adjustments to her mountain environment. As a city dog raised at a kennel in Richmond, she'd never climbed more than a foot above sea level in her first two years of life. Now in the unpaved wilds of Whistler, she got sore pads from the sharp rocks and was spooked by running water. I eventually taught her to ride in the canoe with me as I paddled across Nita Lake. At first she would eagerly leap from the boat when we approached the shore and spill me, and on one occasion my dad, into the glacier-fed water. Eventually I taught her to sit still, wedged in the narrow bow of the boat where she acted as excellent ballast in high winds, until I was ashore and she was given the signal to disembark. It wasn't long before her pads toughened, her fears of the elements vanished and she became a St. Bernard worthy of carrying a brandy keg under her drool-ing chin. But back to the rocks.

In front of Tyrol Lodge stands Tyrol Rock, a square chunk of granite that juts upward like a miniature Stawamus Chief or Rock of Gibraltar. It has some challenging climbs on the lakeside face that are usually tackled by climbers with ropes. On one of our explorations Matt started free climbing, and I followed. He was at the top in short order while I was slowing down with each foot- and handhold. When I got about halfway up (okay, maybe only a third), I got stuck. The next handhold was farther than I was willing to lunge for, and like a cat in a tree, going down proved harder than going up. After a pro-longed interval with me perched on the face, Matt reluctantly

It didn't take long for the young Voglers to emulate the local ski-bum culture at their "Explosives" shack next to the Tyrol Lodge, spring 1977. (Stephen on roof, Peter below and friend Geoff Morrison) PHOTO COURTESY THE AUTHOR

walked up to my house to get help. It may have been the potential embarrassment of being plucked from the rock by family members, or simply having the time alone to gather my wits, but I climbed down from the cliff on my own and called off the rescue mission, at least partially saving face.

My next initiation to life in the mountains involved an off-season gondola evacuation. Robbie Thibeault had an older sister and brother about the same ages as my own siblings. His mom was in and out of town and his dad, Ray, was and still is one of the most unique and bizarre characters to ever grace this valley. Me, Robbie, Matt and Brook Calder, whose parents owned the 76 gas station and the adjacent Food Plus with the aforementioned pinball machines, wandered over to the gondola barn one fall afternoon when we spotted cars running.

Somebody knew Germaine Degenhardt, the valley gondola barn liftee, and soon we were riding up to midstation—one of the perks of being a young, local mischief-maker. Being an avid skier, I'd ridden in these little four-passenger sardine cans hundreds of times, but only when there'd been snow on the ground.

As soon as we disappeared over the first knoll, my new friends started to show me the tricks of the trade, putting the gondola through tests that neither Garibaldi Lifts Ltd. founder Franz Wilhelmsen nor manufacturer Mueller Lifts of Austria had ever considered. One of my buddies had managed to equip himself with the gondola door key as we'd sailed out of the barn, waving innocently to Germaine. Another reached under the seat and produced a coiled nylon string used for gondola rescues. The boys trolled the string through the bushes and small trees that were passing below, snagging them whenever possible to demonstrate the joys of a wildly swinging gondola.

As we approached the highest part of the ride, where the gondola passes over a section of the World Cup downhill course known as the Sewer, my partners in crime prepared for their pièce de résistance. There are different stories as to how the downhill course got its sewage labels. One tale has it that when an early lift construction worker saw one steep section of the run after it was freshly blasted, he suggested that they build a row of outhouses because the skiers would almost certainly shit their pants. Thus the Toilet Bowl was born. By extension the long, straight, tucking section below naturally became the Sewer. Another story claims that the Toilet Bowl got its name from the rotten egg aroma of Howe Sound's Woodfibre pulp mill, detectable during particularly low-pressure southwesterlies. My friends and I were about to provide yet another possibility.

Travelling high above the ski run with only a couple of

minutes left in our ride, somebody opened the door. "Are you ready, Robbie?" one of our crew asked. Apparently he was. With his pants down at his ankles, he flew out the door, one hand on the handle attached to the gondola, the other on the end of the swinging door, his face creased with furrows of concentration. The Sewer and Coach's Corner loomed below as Robbie, hero of the moment, miraculously and successfully managed to evacuate a couple of turds onto the ski run. Cheering, we pulled him back in and quickly shut the door as he pulled up his pants. A moment later we sailed into the midstation gondola barn where Harvey Fellows, or perhaps it was Rob Webster, both liftees of long standing, looked at us slightly askance as we disembarked.

The fall days of exploring the valley and making new friends soon gave way to a Halloween snowfall of the kind that inevitably melts the following day. By December the valley's social scene was focused on Alta Lake and remained there most of the winter. I believe it was sometime in the new year that I walked forlornly across the ice, plaintiff strains of Cat Stevens songs cycling through my head, nursing a broken heart at the loss of my grade seven sweetheart, Lori McNaught. After "going around" for the first half of the school year, things fell apart in a kind of girlfriend exchange gone bad (the grade seven version of wife swapping, I suppose—it was the seventies after all). Oh, how I felt the depths of those cold dark waters yawning beneath the ice of Alta Lake. In the end, I suppose neither childhood nor the cold Arctic front could last forever. By March the snow finally began to fall. Up on the mountain I could at least work out some of my teenage angst and confusion doing the one thing that came naturally to me: skiing moguls.

Whistler was entering its own adolescence. The plans were laid and the sewer pipes in place to accommodate the massive changes that were to take place over the next two decades. That kind of investment in infrastructure hasn't happened again until now, as I write this and the town prepares for the 2010 Olympics. A new athletes' village is under construction, once again on a garbage dump; the sewage treatment plant is being expanded and upgraded; a new water treatment plant and water main are under construction just down the road from where I sit; a full-fledged highway now runs up the Callaghan Valley south of town, accessing a Nordic centre and a potential golf course development; a $100-million sliding centre occupies the base of Blackcomb Mountain, presided over by the new, $50-million Peak 2 Peak gondola. And all of this infrastructure will colour the character of the town over the coming years, likely necessitating further development just to keep the machine fed.

What still strikes me about the winter of 1976–77 was that the older, more innocent Whistler stood side by side with the ambitious new resort on equal footing, enjoying a game of shinny together on the ice of Alta Lake. And what occasionally frightens me is the thought of how today's youth, including my own three wonderful kids, might be testing the worthiness of the latest round of infrastructure expansion.

2

SQUATTERS AND BUSES

One of Whistler's most treasured scraps of lore is that Whistler Village was built on what was once the town's garbage dump. Long before it became home to our trash and a few generations of hungry bears, and even before it was logged in the early twentieth century, the area was a high-bench alluvial forest fed by the mineral-rich glacial silt of Fitzsimmons Creek, which, like a less predictable Nile, occasionally jumped its banks.

How the village site became a garbage dump is a story worth noting, as it combines two eras of the town and is bound together by Whistler's penchant for partying. Florence and Andy Petersen, neighbours of mine along the west side of Alta Lake, have a wealth of stories from the early days in the valley. It was in 1963, they told me, when the plans for Garibaldi Lifts Ltd. were in the works, that speculators and opportunists began arriving at Rainbow Lodge on Alta Lake to scout out the area.

"They all started dumping their garbage in old sheds beside Rainbow and Alta Lake Station, and it ended up all over the place," Florence remembered. "We went to Valleau's logging camp and got some of those forty-five-gallon drums, painted them green—I guess you could say it was Whistler's first green project—and wrote ALSOTS across the side." ALSOTS was the acronym for the tip fund from the Rainbow Lodge's formidable Saturday night parties; it stood for Alta Lake Sons of Tipplers Society. A tippler is "one who drinks (alcoholic) beverages frequently and habitually" and a sot is "a habitual drunk" so the acronym was doubly appropriate. Along with the considerable volume of garbage left behind by the newcomers, the already healthy tip fund had also begun to swell. After cleaning up the original mess, members of the Alta Lake Ratepayers Association began discussions with the province around ideas for a dumping ground. The future village area was deemed suitable because not only had it been logged, but also it sat on a flood plain, which meant it could never be developed. A lease agreement was entered into with the province, and the ALSOTS fund paid for transporting those green barrels across the valley to the new dumpsite.

The fact that the area did eventually see hundreds of millions of dollars worth of development is testimony to the power of well-chosen words. Intent on establishing Whistler's central new village at the base of Whistler and Blackcomb, the council of the day presented their village design plans to the province with the euphemism "training wall" in place of the word "dyke." This, along with the fact that the information was buried in the middle of the document, fondly referred to by staff as the "comic book," convinced Victoria's bureaucrats that the site was suitable for a tourist village.

Squatting at Ground Zero

Some early human inhabitants were already established on the Fitzsimmons flood plain before it became one of BC's most conducive locales for a pub-crawl. I sat down one afternoon with Andy Munster and his wife Bonnie in their house on Balsam Way, to learn about Andy's pre-Bonnie days of squatting next to Fitzsimmons Creek. In 1971 Andy drove his MG sports car across the country from Sherbrooke, Quebec, and arrived in Whistler in September. He did some roofing work, pumped gas at the 76 station, chopped firewood and monkey-wrenched on the MG to keep it running. He also skied, getting to know many of the weekenders from Vancouver who'd built places in Whistler and making connections that would serve him well in his later role as a builder of fine homes.

By 1974, with the housing situation as tight then as it is now, Andy decided to build a squatter's cabin on Crown land. He explained why the Fitzsimmons fan seemed a good location: "It was already cleared so we weren't chopping trees down. And the water was a big thing. We were beside the overflow channel so we brought it up with buckets. Eventually we built a little waterwheel system. We knew it was all temporary, that we wouldn't acquire it through squatters' rights because it was a flood plain." The-dyke-is-really-a-training-wall game was only being played in official circles back then, and Andy's cabin was not just on the flood plain, but practically in the centre of the watercourse. "The house was right where the bike jumps are beside the overflow channel," Andy said. "It could still be standing there today, though you'd see it from the parking lots. Our outhouse was right where the skate park is now."

The beauty of building a stone's throw away from the dump is that you have ready access to a supply of building materials. The sixteen-by-twenty-four-foot two-floor building was framed almost entirely from discarded wood that Andy salvaged before it was plowed under. The porch was built from lodgepole pines, the windows were recycled (they needed some new panes) and the roll-on asphalt roofing brought the total cost to about fifty dollars. "We first heated the place with an airtight stove," Andy recalled, "but then I think it was Seppo Makinen who gave us this wonderful old wood stove. We called it 'Harvey the Wood Pig.' It just gobbled the wood." It took five cords stashed in the adjacent woodshed to keep the house warm through the winter.

Andy Munster's cabin was a social hub for the Fitzsimmons Creek squatters before Whistler Village rose from the nearby garbage dump. PHOTO GREG GRIFFITH

About the time that Andy built his cabin along with friends Randy Cottingham, Dave Pohl and Karen Schneider, other structures were springing up in the same neighbourhood. Earl Carol and his partner Lynn Edwards built about twenty feet away, Brad Sills put up a place nearby, Chico built a geodesic dome across the creek and another cabin went up further downstream. It was the village before the village, and the inhabitants all helped each other out. "Earl would look after things if we went away," Andy recalled. "The firewood thing we'd all do together. We'd go up to Lost Lake where the spar poles were. They left wood they didn't use, and we got about three years' worth out of that."

Squatting wasn't a particularly easy lifestyle, Andy maintained: "We had outhouses. You'd spend at least four or five hours a day dealing with water and heating. Four or five hours you're doing this stuff to survive, on top of bringing in the food and doing the dishes." Rigging up warm showers was one of the squatters' biggest hurdles. In summer they set up a solar shower and in winter their friend Rick Coleman let them use his cabin, known as Rick's Rook, in White Gold. Andy recalled that Rick never asked for money from the squatters who filed through to clean themselves, and who sometimes left behind the odd bottle of Scotch as a thank you.

Life wasn't all hardship on the banks of Fitzsimmons Creek. It was a sociable place with friends stopping in all the time, lots of dinner parties and a couple of big, three-day full-moon bashes with bands and bathtubs full of punch that have etched themselves into Whistler's historic party records. There was the skiing on Whistler Mountain, of course, as well as some bizarre adventures with a 1955 Tucker Sno-Cat that Andy and friends bought from Ski Rainbow, the little bunny hill that once operated north of Alpine Meadows. Hugh Smythe and Mike Collins had their office in White Gold at the time, and they were using their own 1975 Tucker Sno-Cat to mark and tag trails for the soon-to-be-developed Blackcomb Mountain. "We got to know Hugh," Andy said, "and we asked him if it would be all right to take our Sno-Cat up Blackcomb. He said, 'Yeah, go ahead,' so we went up a few times. We'd drive it right across the creek and up the mountain."

The aged Tucker had steel tracks with eighty bearings on each track that needed to be well greased. "That's four times eighty bearings," Andy reminded me. "One time we were up on the mountain and we had to pull one of the tracks off. So we hooked the old track to the hitch. It could slow us down—we thought it would be great. We were coming down the switch-backs and we thought we'd cut one. It was a bit steep. As I went down, the inevitable happened. The whole Cat started tobogganing. I had to park it between two trees or go off a cliff." There were five or six people in the cab and they had to call Hugh for assistance. "They had to cut a whole bunch of trees down and then winch us out," Andy remembered. "That was our last trip up there."

The Tucker also proved useful for valley transportation. "We actually decided to go to the Boot [pub] one time. I think it was a Saturday; the place was full after a big powder day. We drove over the bridge on Nancy Greene Drive then up onto the snowbank at the back of the parking lot. The snow was pitched high. We could see a car here and a car there, but no car in the middle. Perfect. But it turned out there was a Fiat embedded in the snowbank right under our pontoon." Apart from these kinds of incidents, the Tucker did have its benefits for getting its passengers home safely. Its top speed was fifteen miles per hour and there was no way you'd ever get stuck in a snowbank.

Like many others who have made their way in Whistler, Andy got into working construction. He started from scratch with Franz Carpay, one of Whistler's early builders, wheelbarrowing

A good harvest and a water-tight squatter's cabin could keep a ski bum high and dry all winter. PHOTO COURTESY *WHISTLER ANSWER*

Andy Munster and friends embark on one of their (mis)adventures up Blackcomb with their 1955 Tucker Sno-Cat (l–r: Jane Osborne, Andy Munster, unknown, Ralph Hilarood, Michael Leierer, Brian Day, unknown). PHOTO COURTESY *WHISTLER ANSWER*

cement and carrying lumber, and eventually worked his way up to project manager when Franz became busy as a member of Whistler town council. When Franz dissolved the company, Andy partnered with Charlie Davies for a time and then went off on his own, eventually incorporating as Munster and Sons Developments Ltd.

Andy recalled one job toward the end of his squatting days that was easily accessible from his home by the creek. The original Myrtle Philip School had already been built adjacent to the future village and Whistler's recycled town hall, formerly The Keg at Adventures West, had been moved up the hill and put in place across the fields toward Fitzsimmons Creek, where it still stands today. With village plans in full swing, the newly incorporated Whistler Village Land Company needed an office building constructed. They hired Andy and his cohorts. "Every morning we walked across the field to work, these squatters, building this official building for the Land Company," he laughed.

It was a time when two worlds were bumping against each other. As village construction got under way in 1978, the sound of pile drivers could be heard day in and day out from the squatters' cabins, driving steel piles some 125 feet into the sediments of the Fitzsimmons fan to support the village infrastructure and buildings soon to go up. That same year, the Lands Branch in Victoria issued eviction notices to squatters throughout the valley, who at the time comprised at least 10 percent of Whistler's population. The squatters organized themselves, and with *Whistler Answer* publisher Charlie Doyle as spokesperson, petitioned council to support a one-year reprieve that would allow them time to find alternate housing. With eventual support from the town council, the Lands Branch granted the squatters an extension until May 1979 if the occupants of each cabin posted a $500 bond to ensure they would clean up the site after they vacated it.

Even as the eviction notices went up, there were still signs of community and co-operation between the different walks of life in the valley. It was during this era that Whistler Mountain's snow groomers would often stop in at the squat with their Thycol Sno-Cats for a morning coffee. And Andy remembered a gesture of goodwill from the contractor who was constructing the training wall. "We were still driving through the dump. They were building the training wall, but they left us an opening. They made it comfortable for us, it was amazing. When they eventually had to close it up, they said, 'If you want anything out of there, you better get it soon.'" When it came time to tear down the squat, Andy and friends opted to donate it to the volunteer fire department for fire practice. "Before that," he recalled, "we recycled as much as possible, gave things to people who needed them."

The one-year reprieve allowed the squatters at Fitzsimmons Creek, along with others at various enclaves throughout the valley and folks living in more official abodes, to pool their resources and imaginations and come up with a creative housing solution. The collective purchase under the name of Mountain Development Corporation (MDC) of Tapley's Farm, a 106-acre parcel at the foot of Lorimer Road, included many Whistler squatters who wanted to establish a permanent stake in the community and perhaps build a place to raise a family.

"A lot of people who started Easy Street [MDC] were squatters," said Bonnie Munster, who had by then joined forces with Andy. "Harley Paul and Doug Race [two local lawyers with a little more equity than the average squatter] guaranteed everybody's loans. So that was a real community thing. There was a lot of trust and camaraderie." After two years of hard work organizing and lobbying council (whose rezoning approval was finally given, not surprisingly, just before a municipal election), the eighty lots were drawn for at a heady celebration in the

If the walls could talk . . . The old Keg at the Mountain next to Adventures West on Alta Lake was party central before it was moved to the village in the late seventies to serve as Whistler's municipal hall. PHOTO COURTESY CLIFF JENNINGS

Creekhouse Restaurant. Council received eight acres of land for employee housing out of the deal and Whistler got a neighbourhood whose acronym soon stood for Mothers, Dogs and Children. MDC is home to the venerable Easy Street, where a whole generation of local kids has grown up only to encounter the same housing challenges that their parents faced.

Sitting in Andy and Bonnie's house on Balsam Way, I got the same feeling I've experienced talking with other ex-squatters in their Whistler homes: that these families have maintained something essential from their early days of living close to the land. The feeling might stem from the hot water heater rigged up to the wood stove crackling in the entrance-way, the familiar design of the two-storey home with dormer windows that look out on the mountains or the fact that family, friends and visitors come and go through the house at leisure, as though it were some kind of community hostel.

If Whistler can lay claim to a true culture, I believe it comes from living intimately on the land in touch with the elements, and that it reveals itself in the sense of community this way of life engenders. Before the squatters of the sixties and seventies arrived on the scene, Whistler's early pioneers lived a surprisingly similarly existence at Alta Lake. Phil and Dorothy Tapley, who operated Tapley's Farm on the land now occupied by Easy Street, lived happily with a wood cookstove, no running water and an outhouse until 1970; they preferred things that way. That common cultural thread of living close to the land can be traced back to the first inhabitants of this valley as well, the Lil'wat people, who have watched Fitzsimmons Creek jump its banks many times over the centuries.

Andy Munster now designs and builds finely crafted homes for high-end clients under Munster and Sons Developments, the company that he and Bonnie run. Their first masterpiece of sorts was called Akasha, a house that featured a 427-year-old cedar pole, a banister that incorporated a section of steel cable from the old Red Chair and an indoor waterfall. It sold

The squat built by Nigel Protter and Bart Ross stood for ten years on the lower flank of Rainbow Mountain. PHOTO COURTESY NIGEL PROTTER

for $7.9 million in 2000, the most expensive house in the valley at the time. Did his early construction of a squatter's cabin somehow inform these later creations? "Not at all," Andy said with a laugh. But he did talk excitedly about the trend in high-end homes moving toward smaller structures, solar energy and other environmental technologies.

These days Andy's penchant for scavenging materials and throwing up a rustic abode has found another outlet. The Munsters built a boat-access family getaway for themselves and their three sons at McGillivray Falls on Anderson Lake. "It looks surprisingly like the old squat at Fitzsimmons Creek," Bonnie said. "It's totally self-sufficient and off the grid. We thought, if there was ever a disaster we could support ourselves there no problem." A smile started to play on her features. "Then we discovered that during the Cold War, that exact spot at McGillivray Falls was ground zero for a nuclear bomb—I guess because of the power lines that come down to Vancouver and Washington State through there." They may not have chosen the safest location to weather a nuclear winter, but you can't deny that the Munsters have an uncanny knack for divining the very centre of activity.

The Espresso Express
In 1978 two young lads named Nigel Protter and Bart Ross met at one of Andy Munster's full moon parties. Fresh out of high school in Toronto, Nigel had come out to Whistler that summer to see where his neighbour and friend, Jamie Todd, had lived and then died in a house fire at the Snow Castle on Nesters Road. Bart had lived in the same house, and had managed to survive the fire with little more than the shirt on his back. The new acquaintances had a lost friend they shared in common.

Under the influence of the party, perhaps the full moon and certainly the magic mushrooms they'd consumed, Nigel and Bart decided then and there to construct a squatter's cabin of their own. Alta Lake Road on the west side of the valley was much more secluded than Fitzsimmons Creek, and the two found a little shelf of land tucked in the forest beside a creek that burbled down the flank of Rainbow Mountain toward the Emerald Forest. Over the next two months they gathered all the building materials they could find and began transforming them into a sixteen-by-twenty-foot two-storey squat. The boys had a roof over their heads by Halloween and the ski season was on its way. What more could they ask for?

Nigel had saved a little money that summer working for Schultzy the cleaner and as third cook at The Keg, a job that afforded vast amounts of steak and prawns for his nineteen-year-old frame. But getting set up as a ski bum for the winter wasn't enough for him. Nigel attributes his ambitious character to his dad's Austrian Jewish heritage and an inherited sense of obligation to contribute back to the community. It may also have been fostered at Ontario's Upper Canada College, which he grudgingly attended from grades three through ten. "I felt I had to do something constructive, which was start a business. I couldn't just join the UIC [unemployment insurance] ski team and be a ski bum. I had to be an entrepreneur and do something."

That something had already been percolating in his head since the summer. "I had this idea for the cappuccino bus. I realized that people were coming down that [village] side and were waiting around in the cold and rain. Bart was explaining it all to me, and I thought, well, there's an opportunity. I hadn't even skied the mountain yet, though I'd hiked up in the summer to ski in the alpine so I knew the lay of the land.

"In the fall I put together this whole business plan. It was insane because I didn't know what the hell I was doing. But I'd just finished building this house, and I thought, well, if I can do that . . . So I started researching coffee, and I tried to raise money. I went to the Business Development Bank. They turned me down. I was too young and too naïve in their view, I guess."

Nigel returned to his parents and his upbringing to explain why a nineteen-year-old kid would decide to put a cappuccino bus at the muddy foot of Whistler Mountain's Olympic Run. "Both my parents were European. My mother was a Brit and she grew up in a town called Aldershot with an air force base which was heavily bombed during the war. And my dad was an Austrian refugee who fled to Israel. So both my parents had been through that kind of thing and they wanted something better. When they came to Canada they tried really hard to elevate themselves and us as kids. So we were always subjected to the ballet and the opera and good food, you know, people trying to raise the level of culture in their family and around them."

One of the benefits of a boyhood steeped in culture was that Nigel's parents would take him and his three brothers to a little Viennese bakery that served the best cake in Toronto, as well as cappuccino. "We didn't drink the cappuccino, we drank the hot chocolate, but we were constantly exposed to it, to these wonderful pastries and high quality European-style foods. So to me, cappuccino was just something you drank. I didn't realize that no one had heard of it." This was long before Starbucks had swept the known world with tall double skinny soy lattes. Not only had Whistler never seen an espresso or cappuccino, but these rarities could only be found at a few places in Vancouver—the Soft Rock Café on West Fourth and at Continental Coffee and Joe's Café on Commercial Drive.

With nobody willing to loan him money, Nigel approached his father, who backstopped him on a $5000 line of credit. He initially set out looking for a truck, but happened across a bus with a big GM 427 engine that had been written off in an accident and rebuilt. It hadn't been recertified yet, but at $1200 the price was right. Nigel took it from its resting place beside the Lougheed Highway to a do-it-yourself mechanics' garage in Vancouver where he worked on the brakes, replaced the front glass and painted the body with a chocolate brown exterior and a puce interior. The Espresso Express bus looked not only worthy of purveying fine European pastries, but it had begun to resemble one as well.

The next important item was the espresso machine itself. While he was looking for a bean supplier on Commercial Drive, Vancouver's home of fine coffee, the people at Continental Coffee put Nigel in touch with the dealer for Nuova Simonelli espresso machines in Canada. "He helped me out," Nigel remembered. "He said, 'Look, you need a special machine if you're going to put it in a bus.' Normally they go in restaurants where they have two-twenty volts. So he special ordered me a custom-built machine from Italy that could run on one-ten volts or propane." Nigel had clearly found himself an espresso machine designed for a squatter. It was $2300 for the two-group manual machine, nearly twice the cost of the bus that would house it, but it was a beautiful thing, the real deal, Nigel remembers, and it would be the heart of his new business.

Both handy young men and by now fast friends, he and Bart worked on the interior reno of the bus. They turned every second seat backwards, built cabinets, a countertop with a sink, tables that they covered in Arborite and a glassed-in display case. Up in Whistler they got lots of help rigging up the remaining necessities. Darcy the welder built a frame to hold the hundred-pound propane bottle, Charlie Doyle painted the signs and others in the community lent their skills where they could. "There were a lot of people that really helped me out," Nigel said. "Art Den Duyf, Michael D'Artois, Ralph and Denver from Ralph's Towing in Function Junction, Ted Nebbeling and Jan Holmberg. A lot of these older guys were really supportive."

By February 1979 the Espresso Express was open for business. Parked at the bottom of the six-mile-long Olympic Run, it had a steady stream of customers who were more than happy to warm up with a fine coffee and a baked item before catching the other bus back to Creekside. As a teenager I remember emerging from the fog-enshrouded lower run and seeing this beacon of civilization: a hybrid of hippie bus and fine European café with a spectacular view of the landfill. "It was popular right from the start," Nigel recalled. "I can't say I made a fortune at it, but it definitely was an income." And it involved a circle of contributors from the squatters' community who lent their expertise. "Marsha Fladd baked pies and cookies, another woman made soups for me. I had help from all the squatter chicks and hippie chicks around."

After a successful first season, Nigel worked the summer logging out of the Malloch and Mosley camp at Function Junction. When he fired up the bus in the fall of 1979 for another go-round, the local powers began to tighten their bureaucratic

Early days at the propane-powered Espresso Express (l–r: Trish Bongard, Sarah Roncarelli, Kal Protter, Nigel Protter, Adam Protter). PHOTO COURTESY NIGEL PROTTER

The new ski runs on Blackcomb were freshly cut as the Espresso Express still plied its trade at the foot of the Olympic Run. PHOTO COURTESY NIGEL PROTTER

noose. The health inspector decided that the bus required a toilet, which Nigel installed at the expense of one table. (To keep the bus smelling like good coffee rather than an outhouse, he never let anybody use it.) Then the local fire inspector deemed that the bus wasn't in fact a mobile catering unit, as stated in its business licence, because it tended toward immobility. The upshot: it would have to move every ten minutes. And so on. Nigel hired Darcy the welder, who was also a mechanic, to certify the bus so that it could finally get some licence plates. Michael D'Artois, who operated one of Whistler's first bed and breakfasts on Nesters Road, helped Nigel present his case to the municipality, and the Espresso Express eventually managed to steam through another winter.

Nigel recalled a kind of "parking lot culture" that existed at the future village site in those days. The cast of characters included all of the squatters along Fitzsimmons Creek: Andy Munster, Brad Sills, Dana Gow, Lucy, Chico and others; Ray Thibeault, the father of my friend Robbie, who occupied the sunroom in Andy's cabin; a roving heavy-duty mechanic named Julian Soltendieck who lived in his bus in the parking lot; many of Whistler Mountain's ski patrollers—Kathy Jewell, Ken Melamed, Bernie Protsch—who were some of Nigel's best customers; the various bus drivers who transported skiers back to Creekside on the Snow Goose or Milt Fernandez's more ragtag operation out of Pemberton; the larger circle of valley friends Nigel had become a part of, including the publishers of the *Whistler Answer*, Charlie Doyle, Robin Blechman, Tim Smith, Michael Leierer, Jim "Mogul" Monahan and Bob "Bosco" Colebrook; T-shirt Al Davis who lived in his white bread truck from which he silkscreened T-shirts; and a host of other characters.

"It was such a magical time for a young guy. It really was freedom," Nigel said. "You don't realize it until you're older; these guys were real mentors in a way, totally supportive. You thought you were a peer, but you weren't really, you were still a snot-nosed kid, and they were very supportive in the ways that they could be, because they weren't always what you'd call normally functioning people in a typical society. They were definite outliers, but in their own way there were lots of good lessons to be learned, a lot of kindness from those people. I really had very few negative experiences in those days. It was just a magical time."

By the time the Espresso Express was ready for its third winter, Nigel had worked another summer logging for Malloch and Mosley and was ready for a change. He still couldn't see himself becoming a dedicated ski bum. A lot of his ski friends were kids from West Vancouver who had solid family support systems. Nigel had lost his mom and with his dad struggling financially, he needed to make his own way. He rented the Espresso Express to friends Michael Mills and Sara Roncarelli, who operated it even as Whistler Village opened for its first winter. The rent money helped put Nigel through his first year of physical geography at Capilano College. Like a poor young man living the rich man's dream, he had an income stream and a Whistler squatter's cabin to retreat to on weekends.

After its third winter, the Espresso Express continued to carry on in different incarnations. The machine was leased to some people who ran it at the Vancouver Children's Festival one summer. The bus itself went to the Courtenay fair on Vancouver Island with a load of Whistler guys and gals who purveyed more than a few special coffees across the counter. Nigel finally sold the propane-powered two-group Simonelli to Tom Jarvis, who opened Beau's Fine Dining at the base of Ski Rainbow.

Nigel now lives with his partner, photojournalist and painter Karen Love, and their two children in Pemberton. Their house and the hay barn they converted into an artist's studio and office have more than a little down-home warmth to them. Less than a kilometre away, Nigel's friend Bart raises his own family in a wood structure that evokes the charm of the squatter's cabin that miraculously survived until 1987 on the flank of Rainbow Mountain in the Whistler valley.

The Snow Goose

In the late seventies, a most bizarre drama used to unfold at the base of the Olympic Run involving a bus driver and a mess of impatient skiers waiting for a ride back to Creekside. People often chose to ski down the north side of the mountain at the end of a long ski day. It may have been the allure of an undulating, six-mile run that was easier to negotiate with tired legs than Franz's Run or the Gondola Run on the south side, or that paying one's respects to the north side of the mountain offered a sense of adventure and a tour in the European manner of skiing from one village to the next—no matter that the northern village consisted of a garbage dump roamed by hungry bears in the spring, a few long-haired squatters emerging from the woods and a cappuccino bus with a permanently closed bathroom.

When you finally turned the last corner, more often than not dampened by the coastal elements, or alternately toe- and finger-frozen from a persistent high-pressure system out of the north, you were ready to take off your boots and kick back with a hot chocolate or a beer for a well-earned après session. Unfortunately, so were hundreds of others, all waiting for the Snow Goose bus to transport them back to the comfort zone. This was where Ed Gordon came into the picture. Ed drove the Snow Goose bus for Kashi Richardson and Bob Daniels who, among many other transit services they provided in the

One of the larger members of the Snow Goose fleet under a fresh dump of snow at the Creekside base. PHOTO COURTESY KASHI AND BOB DANIELS

valley, leased their buses to Whistler Mountain for the Olympic
Run shuttle. Facing a horde of unruly skiers who had likely
waited in lineups all day, Ed would approach the crowd cau-
tiously. The line control that Whistler Mountain was supposed
to provide was nowhere to be seen. As Ed drew up, the front
lines would grab their skis and shoulder them for an advance
run on his still-moving ski racks. A generally easygoing guy, Ed
wasn't keen on either running over his passengers or having
his windows impaled by their double-edged swords. Instead he
would open his door, yell out an instruction to "Line up, be
orderly!" and step on the gas to circle the parking lot before
returning for another landing attempt. Ed sometimes repeated
this ritual multiple times before the irate and perplexed skiers
were allowed to board the bus. I remember standing among
the eager crowd and, unable in my youth to see the scenario
from the driver's perspective, wondering what sort of madness
had taken hold of his mind.

Kashi drove the bus herself much of the time, and in my
teens I got to know her little by little over brief conversations
on the ten-minute journey back to Creekside. Living proof that
not everyone in Whistler is from Ontario, Quebec or Australia,
Kashi grew up in the Kerrisdale area of Vancouver. She started
trekking up to Whistler with her family on weekends the first
year the mountain opened. In fact, her first ski day was during Christmas holidays in 1965. The mountain wasn't officially open because the Red Chair hadn't been approved yet, but
the gondola took eager skiers up to midstation. The only run
Kashi and her parents could find in the thick fog took them
down to the garbage dump. "After doing the longest snowplow
you've ever done, we had to walk back on the highway to the
Cheakamus Inn carrying all of our gear," Kashi recalled, as I
spoke with her and Bob in their Easy Street kitchen. "I was only

nine years old, carrying these ungainly skis. And one run, that was it, that was your day."

It may have been Kashi's epic trudge down the highway at age nine that set the stage for a bus company that would later ply the same route. "I ended up doing that bus run millions of times," she said with a laugh. "I got to know that two-point-two kilometre distance pretty intimately." Long before the Snow Goose took wing, Kashi was a regular weekend skier with an open invitation to stay at the Whistler Highland condo her older brother bought in 1968.

Bob made his first journey out west from Montreal at the tail end of a university year. He arrived in mid-April 1969 to ski for a few weeks and ended up working at the Christianna Inn on Alta Lake. As the snow melted, the recently built lodge was revealed to be sitting in a huge construction mess and the owner, Sandy Martin, hired Bob and a few others to clean up the grounds and build a dock on the newly formed lagoon. In keeping with a fine old Whistler tradition, the small peninsula jutting into the bay was not a natural geographic protrusion, but a dump site built up to form a land base on which the Christianna Inn could stand.

Bob returned the following fall after another year of university and got a job at the Cheakamus Inn. The owner, John Reynolds, was a likable character who regularly hired a whole crew of young people for the season. Though not a skier, John would reportedly sit around the fireplace during après and regale the guests with stories about the mountain, including the incredible runs on the Purple Chair. The fact that there was no Purple Chair mattered little to the spellbound visitors. Bob lived in a trailer about thirty feet from the hotel with Charlie Davies and Al Gary. "We were handymen, pot washers, you name it. It was $200 a month, room and board, a season's pass and a bar tab. Sometimes the bar tab was more than your

$200," Bob said with a hearty chuckle. "Your exit strategy, though, was that you had a share of the tip fund if you stayed the whole year. If you didn't stay the whole year, you forfeited your share. But the tip fund usually worked out to be between a thousand and twelve hundred bucks by the end of the five months. So that was your ticket to go anywhere."

Bob and Kashi met that December at the Cheakamus Inn and began a long relationship that spawned much travel, a small bus company and two homegrown Whistler daughters, Claire and Mia. It was in 1977 that the two moved back to Whistler full-time to start the bus business. Kashi recalled: "We'd been away travelling in South America and were living in Vancouver and our place was robbed. We just said, 'Oh, let's get out of the city, this is too much.'" The idea for a bus service had already taken root during their travels. In the charming way the two have of trading off a story, Bob took it from there: "When we'd travelled together in South America, you took all forms of transportation down there, and one of them was these little jitney buses, little vans that ran around and took people from A to B. So when we came back to live in Whistler, we were trying to think of some way of making a living and decided that Whistler didn't have a bus service and needed one."

"And also the social aspects of a bus," Kashi added, "where you're in communication with people, you're not isolated in your individual car. It took you out of your capsule, you're all of a sudden having an opportunity to socially interact with people. So that was the other thing." They took out a bank loan to buy a new twelve-passenger van, and with this first member of the Snow Goose fleet, provided not only Whistler's inaugural bus service but also its first taxi. They ran a scheduled route from Emerald Estates in the north to Creekside between 7:00 and 10:30 in the morning, skied in the middle of the day like everyone else, then drove skiers and workers home on the

Long before he and Kashi started the Snow Goose bus, Bob Daniels worked at the Cheakamus Inn in Creekside for $200 a month, room and board, a ski pass and a bar tab. PHOTO MAC LOCKHART

return trips between 2:00 and 5:30. In the evenings they were on call as a taxi service. To keep the van operating and earning its keep, Bob and Kashi came up with other creative ideas. They offered a charter service to and from the Vancouver airport on weekends, as well as Saturday- or Sunday-night "meal and entertainment" trips to the Brackendale Art Gallery, where locals could get a dose of culture for only five dollars, including transportation and cover charge.

Michael D'Artois, who ran the Valley Inn Bed & Breakfast on Nesters Road, was the first business to offer valley transportation as part of a package deal, and it became a regular stop for the Snow Goose. Robin Crumley offered a similar deal for his guests at Tamarisk and Alpine Lodge in Alpine Meadows. Bob and Kashi branched out in other entrepreneurial ways. They not only met the Pacific Great Eastern (later BC Rail) Budd car at the train station in Creekside, but they also shovelled the path, heated the building, put up notices if the train was late and even sold fresh-baked muffins and coffee to waiting passengers. Special trips could be chartered to Vancouver for concerts or hockey games or whatever kind of city trip might interest a bunch of locals who didn't want to drive.

By their second year, Bob and Kashi had expanded the business to meet the growing demand for public transportation in the valley with the first of five second-hand school buses. Kashi recalled being so busy in the second or third year she barely skied at all, and started to wonder why it was they'd moved to Whistler. Their expanding staff included Ed Gordon, Al Schmuck, Peter Grant, Lisa Richardson, Mark Steinberg, Diane "Dianski" Rajinski and other notable long-time locals who appreciated the solid working conditions and fair remuneration. The Snow Goose offered higher wages than most Whistler Mountain jobs and a free season's pass, the first small business in the valley to offer such a deal. The owners even got some perks: "Another

Driver and co-owner Kashi Daniels stands with clients beside one of the Snow Goose buses after a trip to Vancouver. PHOTO COURTESY KASHI AND BOB DANIELS

thing we did in those days was getting some advertising on our brand new van," Bob recalled. "We had Dynastar and Demetre, and the great coup was getting a pair of boots each. I don't think I'd ever had a pair of new ski boots in my life before then, so I thought it was just a great deal."

Maintaining a bus company also involved dealing with three levels of government and endless amounts of red tape for licensing and regulatory permits. Bob recalled his negotiations with the Motor Carrier Commission from Victoria: "We got to know those people down there quite well over the years because there was always an issue and always another hoop to jump through. The one I remember vividly was when we had an inspector come up to inspect one of the school buses that we'd purchased, and he had a stick with him that was either thirty-two or thirty-four-and-a-half inches long, and that was the permissible distance between seats. And of course, in the school bus, the seats were closer together than what they would allow for public transportation, so we had to take out all the school bus seats, redrill and relocate all the seats so that his thirty-two-inch stick would work."

"And he would come up in his street shoes and his suit," Kashi added. "He was a total duck out of water and he didn't have an entrepreneurial bone in his body. He just thought we were out to make money, and he was just collecting his little cheque every month; it's just such a different mindset." In fact, Kashi and Bob didn't make any money for the first couple of years. To subsidize their winter operations, they ran cross-Canada bus and camping trips under the name Orca Tours for European tourists. They also leased their vans to Gray Line of Vancouver and drove tourists from various city hotels to the Hotel Vancouver, which was the departure point for tours of the city. The relationship with Gray Line also enabled Snow Goose to lease larger highway coach buses for their winter airport runs.

The Snow Goose finally began to turn a profit the first year Bob and Kashi got the contract with Whistler Mountain to operate the Olympic Run shuttle. They transported over 150,000 people that winter, but as for operating a scheduled bus service throughout the valley, they began to see that it would never be viable without the support of the municipality. "We travelled down to Vail and all around Colorado," Kashi said, "and did an analysis of what they were doing for bus service, and of course Vail at the time had free inter-valley bus for their people. And what a huge boon that was for tourism, because people knew that they didn't have to deal with a car, and they'd just get around everywhere with the bus—to the lifts, to their hotel, to their restaurants or whatever. Whistler was just so far behind the times, not wanting to put up one penny for any kind of transportation at all. And then the scenario with parking and people bringing their cars into the valley. Even then there were the crowds and chaos on the highway and in the parking areas."

Whistler town council showed no interest in supporting a similar approach to public transit, and Bob and Kashi had no luck trying to get them onside. On top of that, they soon found that the municipality didn't think that the locally based Snow Goose was the right company to provide valley transportation. "They thought we were too local," Bob said, "that the buses, because they were school buses, weren't up to scratch for the new image of the world-class ski resort." While most visitors to a ski town would find a well-run and -maintained fleet of school buses with local drivers one of the charms of their stay, the idea of "world class" had taken hold of both Whistler and Vancouver during the eighties, usually at the expense of promoting local character and colour. "The emphasis was on how things looked," Kashi said. "I think part of what brought us out of the bus business was they needed to have the bus company that looked a certain way, and it wasn't to do with heart and soul or operation or anything. And then so much of what they built had to have a certain look. It's like a restaurant that looks really good and has all the fancy furniture, but the food sucks. What about the quality that goes on in these buildings?"

It was also the era of Blackcomb's new school of guest services. "I think it was with the best intentions, but it was . . . Remember the old Keg Restaurant? 'Hi, I'm your server, my name's . . .' Sorry we didn't really want to know your name," Kashi joked. "It's taken whatever kind of genuine interaction there was—and maybe people weren't super guest-service oriented in the old days—but then it just went totally over the top in the other direction. All of a sudden it was, 'Hey, how's your day going?' for the thirty-fifth time. I mean, a little bit of genuine interaction is great, but if people are happy with where they're living, with the work that they have, the remuneration that they're getting, the ski pass and the skiing, that comes through."

Going into their fourth year of operations with Snow Goose, Bob and Kashi saw that the municipality was courting Gray Line for Whistler's bus service. Bob recalled the turning point: "We thought, okay, we can see the writing on the wall here—the municipality's not going to support our little entrepreneurial venture—so we went to Gray Line, who we already knew from our summertime relationships. We said, 'Listen, we've already got the licence, we'll either sell to you or we'll sell to someone else,' because we knew the licences had some value." Gray Line agreed to buy both the Snow Goose licences and the buses. It was a bittersweet time for Bob and Kashi; after four years of growing the business they'd finally turned the corner and had started to make some money.

It turned out that their hard work didn't go unrewarded. Their decision to sell came at the beginning of an inflationary period when people were paying a premium for everything. On top of that, Gray Line bought out the business over a three-year timeframe, so the unpaid balance was earning double-digit interest for the young couple. "That little deal to sell Snow Goose enabled us to buy a lot in Tapley's Farm and build our house," Bob recalled with satisfaction. "It gave us an opportunity to build a shelter." And the sad irony of Whistler opting for a world-class bus company was that Gray Line went out of business after two seasons, leaving Whistler without public transportation for the next nine years.

Ed Gordon, incidentally, still drives one of Whistler Mountain's shuttle buses, so if you see him approaching, please wait in an orderly fashion.

3

ON DISHWASHING
AND DEAD HORSES

While the roaring inflation of the early eighties would eventually lead to the near-bankruptcy of the Resort Municipality of Whistler, it offered great summer job prospects for a Whistler teenager. The affluence of the summer of 1981 can best be demonstrated by the progression of my summer jobs to that point. In 1979 I worked for the BC Parks Board, cutting a trail a little farther toward Singing Pass each day with a small crew that included two of the Logue brothers from my high school and our foreman, Mike Suggett, who owned a small trail-building Cat. Remuneration for hiking in and out each day and operating a shovel, mattock and rake: $4.18 per hour. The following summer I worked on Blackcomb Mountain, then abuzz with energy in the lead-up to its inaugural ski season. The jobs the trail crew took on involved everything from rolling bucked logs into piles for burning to blasting and then picking rocks out of the trench for the electrical cables to my eventual occupation, helping electrician Gary Carr install the electrical platforms for each of the four chairlifts. When it came to driving the Ford pickup trucks up and down Blackcomb's access road no one seemed concerned about whether you had a driver's licence or not. As a result, both my friend Mark MacLaurin and I managed to put the trucks in the ditch on a few occasions that summer. Remuneration: $6 per hour.

In 1981 Whistler Village was getting ready to host its first summer visitors. The garbage-dump-turned-construction-site/tourist village was in serious need of landscaping and a union company from the Lower Mainland won the contract to adorn the many walkways and planter beds with shrubs and trees. The company seemed willing to hire just about anybody, me and my seventeen-year-old summer cohorts Mark MacLaurin and Owen Walsh included. At its worst, the job involved digging seemingly endless rows of tree holes in the pouring rain. Once the flora was planted, however, we were able to put our new drivers' licences and our previous summer's mountain driving experience to good use. We tootled in and around the village with two or three big water barrels in the back of the pickup truck, stopping every thirty feet or so to water the shrubs and trees while the Clash blasted out of the cab into the glorious sunshine. Remuneration: $12 per hour. As if that wasn't enough to fortify a seventeen-year-old's bank account, Owen and I also both worked washing dishes in the evenings at L'Après restaurant at the base of Whistler. In the interest of full disclosure and to illustrate the kind of largesse that can lead to economic recession (keeping in mind also the seven-year statute of limitations), if one of us occasionally had to start an earlier shift at L'Après, the other would sign out for both at the end of the landscaping day. Illegal remuneration: $18 per hour.

Eighteen dollars per hour seemed like a fair exchange for having to peel a hundred pounds of onions for the Greek's famous pizza after landscaping all day. To back up a little, L'Après was Whistler's first après-ski bar, located at the base of the original Creekside gondola. Leo and Soula Katsuris first opened the cafeteria and lounge in 1966, and were later joined by brother-in-law Peter Skoros and Leo Lucas. By the early seventies when my family started skiing at Whistler, the Greek's thick-crust pizza was famous throughout the valley and beyond. Their menu included other authentic Greek dishes such as moussaka, calamari, Greek salad and saganaki (fried goat cheese). The pizza was so popular that even in the summer it was necessary to peel untold quantities of onions and grate huge bricks of cheese into a mixer the size of a small cement truck. These duties all fell to the dishwasher.

The windows and patio of the L'Après bar looked out over a sprawling vista of Whistler peak, its alpine bowls and southside runs. It was the perfect setting for tired skiers who wanted nothing more than to gaze back up the mountain and relive the day's feats over a pint of beer or a glass of retsina. The sun-drenched patio with its natural surrounding amphitheatre provided a kind of theatre-of-the-absurd for the après crowd. I recall sitting on the patio one spring in the mid-seventies and watching crazed locals drive Jeeps, motorcycles and beaters up the old T-bar cut to see who could get the highest without killing themselves. Over at stage left, the off-load ramp from the Olive Chair delivered spring skiers, often clad in little more than shorts and bikini tops or T-shirts, to their fate on the Green Meanie—a plastic sliding surface that consisted of sharp green blades in round formations specially designed to tear the skin from the unsuspecting. A theatre director couldn't have created a better mix of drama and comedy as two by two the disembarking skiers performed a comic ballet. Those who made it to the flats at the bottom were often quickly separated from their skis by a much softer and slower green carpet that could cause a sudden stop followed by an instantaneous double heel release. To add insult to injury, local ski instructors and other miscreants lined up at the bottom of the ramp with scorecards, awarding points for both elegant execution and creative destruction.

I once witnessed a most extraordinary scene just below the off-load ramp, in the courtyard between L'Après and the Gondola Barn. It was late morning, on one of those days when the freezing level rises above the valley floor, leaving grey rain and puddles in place of a winter wonderland. Ray Thibeault was kneeling in one of those puddles, his ski equipment draped around him as he stared at the money in his hands, perhaps his change from a lift ticket purchase. "Money—it's so fucking weird," he said with a mystified laugh. Some might have simply concluded that Ray was stoned out of his mind, but I've always wondered if his pronouncement didn't foretell some of the many changes that "weird" stuff would bring to the valley over the next couple of decades. But back to L'Après.

While the front of the building was a wide open segue to the outdoors, the back concealed a labyrinth of hallways, storerooms and small, windowless offices behind the kitchen. It was here that I spent my summer evenings rifling pizza-encrusted plates into the steaming menace of a dishwasher. The head cook at this Greek restaurant was George, a small Chinese man who, as far as I could tell, knew seven words of English, all of them indecipherable. When he sent me to the storeroom for a particular ingredient, it usually took me several tries before I emerged with the correct one.

With Whistler Village opening brand new nightclubs, including The Mountain House (now Tommy Africa's), The Brass Rail (Savage Beagle) and Club Ten (Maxx Fish), L'Après at the southside made a concerted effort to stay in the game of Whistler's burgeoning nightlife scene. To this end, they installed a raised dance floor, coloured lights and a mirror ball for Saturday disco nights at Le Club. Ex-ski instructor and current ski-boot fitter extraordinaire John Colpitts spun the discs, and the place was usually packed and moving en masse to the B52s and other slightly retro music. Knowing the intricacies of the labyrinthine back hallways and being on good terms with the doorman, I was able to attend some of these festivities. I recall dancing with girls who were sometimes a head taller, and occasionally more under-aged, than myself. As it turned out, I didn't need to look even as far as the disco for romance. It was a young L'Après waitress up from Richmond for the summer who, by the end of that season, had ushered me out of adolescence and into young manhood.

Dusty's

At the end of the 1982–83 ski season, L'Après served its last pizza. The Greeks, who had also run the food service in the Roundhouse on top of the mountain, ended their long tenure with Whistler Mountain and took their famous pizza recipes to Peter's Underground in the village. That summer I worked for Whistler's building maintenance department, which was run by my dad, Heinz Vogler, known on the mountain as Your Heinzness. During that period my family had the good fortune of living in the mountain manager's house next door to the gondola barn. There were a few years in the early eighties when the whole family was employed by Whistler—my brother and sister and I as ski instructors, my dad as the building maintenance manager and my mom, Betty, doing cash accounting in one of Whistler Mountain's little offices behind L'Après. It was highly convenient to roll out of bed, walk a few steps across the bridge over Franz's Creek and upload the gondola for a ski lesson.

One of the jobs for building maintenance in the summer of 1983 was renovating L'Après. I worked with Ski School directors Bob Dufour and Don Barr tearing out the old panelling and replacing it with drywall, and ripping out the dance floor and DJ booth, while others cleaned and refurbished the kitchen. The kitchen cleaning crew uncovered some archeological evidence of fifteen-odd years of operation behind stoves and coolers, objects that will forever remain in the realm of mystery. While the renovations were underway, an antiques salvage company scoured the west coast of the US for odd bits of Wild West memorabilia. This style of decor may not have had any connection to the Whistler valley, but stuffing old things into bars and restaurants was in vogue at the time. An interior designer went along for the ride and came back with piles of stained-glass windows, a giant metal sign of a flying horse, a hefty wooden bar with a big crack that my dad got his carpenters to repair and the obligatory metal washtubs and scrub boards. The centrepiece of the collection, however, was Dusty, a famous 1920s bronco from Texas that had been stuffed in a bucking position. Dusty was saddled up and placed in a corner of the bar. I have since learned that Dusty's renown was worthy of earning him a place in a rodeo museum. With the renovations complete and the Western movie set fully installed, the old wooden "L'Après" sign was taken down from the outside wall facing the skier parking lot and replaced with a "Dusty's" sign to usher in the new era.

Whistlerites took to the Western theme and to the free barrels of peanuts that patrons were encouraged to shell and discard on the floor (this was before the age of peanut allergies, though quite possibly the cause of their later proliferation). There was a new energy and excitement at Whistler Mountain, which was now in its first few years of competition with neighbouring Blackcomb. Blackcomb strongly promoted a new brand of customer service that, while raising the bar for on-mountain service, was infused with a certain "Would you like fries with that?" quality. The recycled Old West theme somehow better suited the tone of the refurbished Whistler Mountain, with its three new chairlifts emerging from the village. At a time when so much in the valley was shiny new, Dusty's charm lay in the fact that even the newly installed drywall and flooring couldn't conceal its age and character.

From its inception, Dusty's became the backdrop for many bizarre and humorous local stories. Most of Whistler Mountain's employees, from vice-presidents and managers down to liftees and dishwashers, were still based out of the Creekside, so the bar patrons were a mix of all levels of staff and the general skiing public, many of them long-time weekend skiers from Vancouver. Lorne Borgal, previously Hugh Smythe's right-hand man at Blackcomb, had recently been scooped up as Whistler's new president. Not to be outdone by Her Majesty the Queen, Lorne had paper money printed with his picture on it. Employees could purchase Borgal Bucks at a 40 percent discount, and use them to buy food and beverages at mountain establishments. Just prior to Dusty's grand opening, Lorne also lured Blackcomb's Shelley Phelan over to Whistler as the new marketing director.

Bob Dufour, then director of the ski school and now vice-president of operations, recalled how Dusty's opening unfolded. "Lorne Borgal invited all the dignitaries from town, the mayor and council, the clergy, everybody. Shelley was new on the job, not even a month. Later in the evening, I guess she'd had a few drinks, she got on the horse and took off her top. Everyone thought it was good fun. It was typical of Whistler at the time," Bob said with a chuckle. "A great way to open the bar."

The Lady Godiva incident took on such mythic proportions

in the valley that over twenty years later Shelley finally found it necessary to write a letter to *Pique Newsmagazine* to clarify what really happened: "A staff party had taken place the night before, at which a female staff member had ridden the horse, fully clothed," Shelley wrote. "I had recently been hired as Whistler Mountain's marketing manager, a single, twentysomething female on an otherwise all-male management team, most of whom were about twice my age. Unable to attend the staff party the night before, I heard all about the horse-mounting incident many times over at the Grand Opening, and was encouraged by many to follow suit, which I eventually did. Some of my fellow management team then persuaded me to ride the horse 'bareback.' In the spirit of fun, and in a naïve burst of 'what-the-heck' exuberance, I obliged them. And the rest is (somewhat distorted) history, which continues to amaze and amuse me to this day."

She agreed with Bob Dufour that it was a great way to open the bar. "I still maintain that it was a stroke of marketing genius, however unintentional it may have been at the time," said Shelley. "There is nothing I could have done to raise the profile of Dusty's overnight any more effectively than ride that horse, and twenty-three years later they're still talking about it!" The only part of the oft-told story that irks Shelley is the inaccuracy that she'd been fired for her actions. While she did receive a stiff warning from Lorne Borgal for her "performance," she remained marketing director for another eighteen months and left of her own volition to pursue other opportunities after successfully coordinating Whistler's twentieth anniversary celebrations.

While Dusty's debut was spectacular, the eventual demise of both the bar and the horse provided even more epic tales. It was in the late 1980s that the bar was spruced up again and Dusty was put out to pasture. He was initially auctioned off to raise money for a local charity. Sue Ross, a ski instructor who had worked on the cleaning crew during L'Après' renovation, became intimately entwined with Dusty's journey from the bar. "He went on a kind of fundraising circuit," she recalled. The steadfast horse had already raised money for various local organizations by the time Sue and her husband Bart (squatting partner of Nigel Protter) showed up at an event in Dusty's for the Whistler Winterhawks hockey team. "Someone from the Winterhawks had donated it," Sue said. "There was a dingleball car in need of repair, a broken fridge full of beer and Dusty the dead horse." While most agreed the broken fridge was the top prize, Sue had her eye on the horse for its vintage saddle with carved rosettes and a brass horn. "I'd just bought a place in Pemberton and bought my first horse. I said, 'I need that saddle.'" She was already mak-

Bart and Sue Ross take Dusty for a ride after winning the infamous bronco and his saddle in a *Let's Make a Deal* fundraising contest at Dusty's. PHOTO BRIAN HYDESMITH

ing plans to offer some cash to the winner following the *Let's Make a Deal*-style contest. But as luck and karma would have it, Sue and Bart won Dusty fair and square through the luck of the draw. "It turned out they picked our number. I went 'Yahoo!' We went outside, got our picture taken with the horse and promptly got loaded."

Sue and Bart took the saddle home and said they'd get the horse the next day, but Dusty never reached his destination. "Some guy phoned the next morning from Vancouver and said 'I heard you won the bucking horse. My friend's in Europe. I want to put the horse in his yard when he comes back.'" Sue was ready to make a deal. She was watching *Timmy's Telethon* on TV at the time and in light of Dusty's past fundraising successes, she said he could have the horse if he made a donation to the telethon in Dusty's name. "I was watching and it came on screen: 'ONE HUNDRED DOLLARS FOR DUSTY THE DEAD HORSE.'" The fact that the guy never picked up his horse left Sue as the point person for Dusty's ongoing adventures. "The mountain called and said, 'Sue, your horse is still in the bar.' And I said, 'It's not my horse.'"

Members of the ski patrol eventually carried Dusty to the Volly Patrol cabin on the hillside next to the mountain manager's house. "They set it up beside Honest Eddie, the pop machine turned beer machine," Sue said, "and they'd pay a dollar and have a beer with Dusty, maybe ride him bareback occasionally." One spring evening, some staff members took him up the mountain for a little open-range adventure. Dusty rode up the gondola on a transport car, then probably up the Pony Trail on the back of a groomer. At the top, the pranksters hoisted him up onto the lift evacuation practice tower next to the alpine office. Bob Dufour, silent witness to a few of Dusty's adventures, was riding up the Red Chair on a Monday morning and saw the horse high in the sky. "It was something to see," he recalled. Other observers, some with animal rights concerns, complained about the inappropriate treatment of a dead animal. According to Sue, Bob phoned her and said, "Sue Ross, get your horse off the tower."

It was about this time that Dusty began to enter the realm of mythology. Missing a leg now, it was rumoured that the horse spent a year slowly making his way across the Northwest Passage, an old logging road that traverses the lower flank of Whistler Mountain from Creekside to the village. The journey has a nice ring to it for a busted-up busting bronc, but in fact

Dusty headed for Blackcomb Mountain on the Mini Spearhead Traverse. My brother-in-law, Ian Bunbury, long-time Whistler Mountain ski patroller and curator of the Ski Patrol Bomb Shack Museum, recalled the midnight snowmobile journey to the Dark Side, as Whistler stalwarts sometimes referred to Blackcomb. "We didn't want to be seen by the administration offices on the lower road, so we took the Mini Spearhead Traverse," said Ian. Like an injured skier after an ill-fated "last run," Dusty rode in the ski patrol toboggan, limbs akimbo, the spray of April corn snow wreaking havoc on his weathered hide. "He was in rough shape, starting to fall apart," Ian recalled. "I think his head even fell off at one point." An experienced searcher for lost skiers in the backcountry, Ian had to admit that he, his brother Paul and a few other accomplices got a bit lost that night after crossing the bridge over Fitzsimmons Creek. It was Dusty's dark night of the soul. As they climbed the service road on Blackcomb, keeping a scout on the lookout for groomers all the while, the spring snow eventually got too deep for the snowmobile to complete Dusty's ascent. While they'd wanted to perch him high in the alpine for one last salute to the Coast Mountains, they had to settle for the top of Chair No. 2, about halfway up the mountain. There Dusty was mounted at the top of the liftee shack, ready to greet the morning skiers and raise Blackcomb's commitment to customer service to a whole new level. Found in his ragged state the next morning, Dusty was quickly sent down the mountain to the parking lot, a fate not unlike that of any unshaven liftee who'd been out boozing the night before.

Tattered, torn and jobless, Dusty was sent packing to the Whistler garbage dump at Function Junction. Even with the little time he had left in this world, Dusty's capacity for inspiring hijinks remained intact. Different versions of the story attribute different names to the characters who played a role in

Dusty's ignominious garbage dump journey, but perhaps it's best to leave names out of it when the police become involved. This much we know: Dusty's chauffeur had the horse in the back of the pickup truck en route to the dump for a final burial. Turning off the highway and making his or her way up the gravel road, the thought of dumping a once-famous museum-worthy equine in the landfill was too much for the driver to bear. As the truck stopped on the old log bridge over the Cheakamus River, Dusty made one last jump for freedom. "Give me the pure fresh water of the mighty Cheakamus," I can still hear him whinnying, "to the smelly refuse of a rapidly growing world-famous ski resort any day."

Dusty was still being washed by the cold back eddies of the Cheakamus River at Function Junction when a kayaker spotted the dead horse in the water and called the RCMP. They brought in a dive team and soon called a crane to pull the horse from the river where it had clearly stumbled over the rugged bank to its death. "After winching it out with great effort, energy and expense," Sue Ross explained, "the Mounties called on local cowboy, Layton Bryson, who ran the horse stables at Mons. There was a brand on the horse's rear end and they wanted to identify what ranch it originated from." Layton took one look at the horse and the brand and apparently said, "That's Dusty. He's been dead for fifty years." The RCMP officers didn't find the situation particularly humorous; they wanted to press charges. Sue was called upon once again, and had to explain that if need be she could contact *Timmy's Telethon* to confirm that the horse no longer belonged to her.

Dusty made one final journey from the Cheakamus River back to the parking lot at Blackcomb's Base II. There, he left this world in a final blaze of glory that involved a can of gasoline and a match. Compared to rotting in Whistler's landfill, Dusty's funeral pyre ending was a far more fitting close to his life, two lives really, steeped in adventure, mischief and self-less giving. A belated obituary, *The Deadhorse*, later appeared in a supplement to the *Whistler Question* and offered a partial account of Dusty's trails in Whistler. No doubt other versions of the story will continue to emerge in the future, testament to the unbridled myth-making capacity of Dusty the twice-dead horse.

Sue has ridden in Dusty's saddle for eighteen years and counting. She has had some of the leatherwork repaired, which lessened the antique value, although someone once offered her $500 for it. The president of Whistler Mountain contacted Sue in the late nineties when they were designing the new Dusty's Bar. They wanted to install the saddle along with other Whistler-based memorabilia including an old gondola and black-and-white ski photos. "I said I'd donate it back if they would donate $3000 to the Disabled Ski Program," Sue recalled. "He said, 'Yeah, yeah, I'll get back to you.' but never did." Sue has used the saddle in many fashion magazine layouts in her work as a shoot director, and it sometimes makes appearances at Western-themed parties. "I put saddle boots beside it with flower plants in them," she said. "I'm just waiting for someone to buy it, maybe during the Olympics, to raise money for the Disabled Ski Program." It would be a nice way for Dusty, now gone from beneath his old saddle, to ride off into the sunset and keep on giving.

The Last Stand

To bring the original Dusty's Bar to its rightful end, I must jump ahead to spring 2000. In that millennial year, Whistler Mountain, now owned by Blackcomb parent company Intrawest, was ready to rebuild the entire Creekside base area. All the old buildings would be flattened that summer to make way for new base facilities, a cluster of shops and the highly

Party politics! Local gals Kelly Nylander and Pat Rowntree, disguised as the Jonies, lament the destruction of Whistler's oldest watering hole at Dusty's Last Stand. PHOTO COURTESY DUSTY'S BAR

lucrative condominiums that would surround it all. A grand closing party was called for, and it was dubbed Dusty's Last Stand.

Dusty's had been the scene of some great parties during its seventeen years of existence, thirty-four years if you include its L'Après days. There were Cinco de Mayo parties, Ullr Fests, New Year's Eve celebrations, Rob Boyd's retirement party and a host of others that stand out in their sheer ability to tax the memory. One of my favourite events took place in 1994 after a World Cup downhill race. That was the winter my son Jonathan was born, and I'd managed to get up the mountain for a rare day of skiing. Though I'd started out my day in the village, when I got to the turnoff at Lower Franz's, something pulled me toward the old Creekside. As I rounded Franz's Hop, the last knoll of the downhill course, I heard the strains of the Satellites, a reggae band from Toronto, drifting up the mountainside. The band was set up under a huge tent from which hundreds of people spilled out into the courtyard, all celebrating the successful completion of a World Cup downhill. Grins were written across the band members' faces as local girls danced on picnic tables alongside stuffy European race officials who were disarmed by the happy party vibe. The tent sometimes lifted slightly above the band, possibly from the ganja smoke, the positive energy or the deep bass notes. Whether you were a dog, a child or a senior citizen, it was impossible to leave and equally impossible not to dance. My wife Peggy arrived a little later with Jonathan strapped into his Snugli. They both danced to the reggae rhythms as the baby was initiated into the festivities of a legendary Whistler après party.

When April 2000 rolled around, it wasn't easy for dyed-in-the-wool locals to say goodbye to their favourite watering hole. There were so many fond memories wrapped up with the building that the stories themselves seemed to be holding the place together. In its last few years it had begun to resemble a ghost-town building. A leaky roof occasionally dripped onto the pool table that slanted north at an acute angle. As local columnist G.D. Maxwell recently pointed out to me, it was the only bar in town that required a system of indoor eavestroughs. Creekside dogs ran through the place as though they owned it. The chipped cement of the patio had long been sun-bleached white and the dust would blow up from the gravel parking lot, coating the sunglasses-clad revellers in a thin residue, not unlike the mummified remains of Pompeii.

For some, the entire winter of 2000 was a kind of slow farewell to Dusty's. For me it started on New Year's Eve when the band my brother Peter and I fronted, the Hounds of Buskerville, were hired to ring in the new millennium at Dusty's. At ninety-nine dollars a head, it was one of the least expensive parties in town and therefore attracted many locals. Apart from promoting price-gouging in Whistler and elsewhere, the turn of the millennium also brought with it fears of the computer meltdown known as Y2K. As the evening progressed toward the magic hour, generators and candles were at the ready to get us through the crash of Western civilization as we knew it. As it turned out, the lights and amplifiers stayed on and the party carried on into the wee hours, stopped finally not by a software glitch but by the onset of numbness in our drummer's feet.

Dusty's Last Stand had been well publicized as the party to end all parties. On the Saturday night Tom Lavin's Powder Blues Band played the last of their many gigs over the years in the old bar. On Sunday a series of local bands played throughout the afternoon under a tent on the patio, with the Hounds of Buskerville, still in favour at that point with the management, having the honoured position of playing last. It was a perfect sunny spring day and as the skiers and boarders slid down the old southside, the crowd of revellers gradually increased.

Catou Crookshank, a coach with Whistler Gymnastics, was a Dusty's waitress at the time. "It was pretty crazy," she said of the Sunday afternoon bash. "Just the memories flooding back of doing circles, and then slowly my circles got bigger and bigger up the hill as more and more people arrived." Another waitress was pregnant and after a few hours Catou had to take over her area as well. "People were giving me gifts because it was the last time I'd serve them. I remember selling crazy amounts of booze. It was all just five-dollar drinks. My total sales were $2500 plus. I just had tons of money stuffed in my apron. It started falling out and friends would help stuff it back in. I finally went back to my manager and said, 'Can I do something about this?' She said, 'Oh yeah,' and gave me a bag and then she put it in the safe." As the afternoon wore on, the snowy amphitheatre-of-the-absurd filled up with thousands of people. Some were on the roof holding up farewell signs to Dusty's. Assistant manager Kelly McGuire recalled: "At one time both

The crowd gathered throughout the afternoon and into the night to give Dusty's and Whistler's original Creekside base a raging send-off. PHOTO ROD HARMAN

Hughs [Mayor Hugh O'Reilly and Intrawest President of Resort Operations Hugh Smythe] were on the roof and I had to ask them to get down." A streaking local snowboarder rode into the mayhem and was promptly arrested by the RCMP.

"It was kind of funny because the inside of Dusty's was absolutely empty all day long," Catou remembered, "and then you just snapped your fingers and inside was packed and outside was empty, because I guess the sun went down and it got cold. The lineups for the bar were to the back door." A lot of people couldn't fit in the bar or the tent, and the parking lot turned into a big tailgate party as well. While the computers had survived the change over to the year 2000, they decided that the afternoon of Dusty's Last Stand was a good time to break down. The servers huddled in the side bar known as the Den waiting for the computers to be repaired so they could cash out and start partying with the rest of the hooligans.

Having partaken in the sunny patio action, I'd gone home to meet the rest of the band members who'd driven up from Vancouver for the event. My brother-in-law Ian, travelling mate of Dusty the dead horse, met us at the bar with his camera to capture Dusty's send-off on video. With a good eye for history, Ian followed us through the labyrinth of hallways behind the kitchen (picture *Spinal Tap* set in Whistler Creek instead of Cleveland). He captured the old cooking implements, the huge mixers and coolers that had kept three-and-a-half decades of après skiers happily fortified. Then we emerged into the bar where it was virtually impossible to move, and equally difficult to get a drink. There were still a couple of bands to go before we would play so we put our instruments behind the stage under the big patio tent and grabbed a beer.

As our time in the limelight approached, the bar manager informed me that things were getting too crazy and he might have to close down the party before we played. Having seen the

Local girls celebrate in style at Dusty's Last Stand, April 2, 2000. PHOTO ROD HARMAN

poster for the event that advertised "All Day All Night" and "The Party Lives On," this seemed a rather lame approach for a final send-off to Whistler's oldest après bar. Fortunately, he regained his fortitude and stayed with the loosely written script. After all, there was still some beer to sell and a few liquor regulations that hadn't been broken yet. The afternoon crowds had been squeezed down to under two thousand now, not including the raft of tailgate parties that had cropped up in the parking lot.

I can honestly say that our final gig at Dusty's was more fun than a tent full of drunken monkeys, and it was only a little terrifying to stand on stage in the midst of it all. Some time during our set, people started launching themselves off the stage into the mosh pit. I was busy trying to keep the microphone from dislodging my teeth and got a better view of the stage divers later on Ian's video. He also trained the camera at times on Dusty's manager Paul Street, who stood beside the stage looking increasingly nervous and ready to pull the plug at any moment. Our drummer, Graham Wilkins, had brought his dad Rick and sister Beth along to appreciate this historic event. Rick Wilkins is one of Canada's finest jazz composers and arrangers.

A member of the Boss Brass, he has played with and arranged for the world's best jazz musicians including Oscar Peterson, whom Graham remembers would often stop by for breakfast at the Wilkins household when he and his sisters were growing up in Toronto. Rick Wilkins had just one thing to say after Dusty's Last Stand: "I'm glad I got to witness that before I die."

I like to think that if the guitar and bass amplifiers had been in some other spot on stage things might have transpired differently. As it was, when I turned over the vocal mike to my brother and started to play bass, I had a very short range of motion. As our set progressed I looked over at Paul and saw him signalling us to wrap it up. After one more song he was dragging his fingertips across his throat in a gesture that meant either "stop playing now," or "I'm going to kill you when you finally get off the stage." I started to walk over to him for clarification, but the length of my guitar cable stopped me short. Okay, I'll admit the fact that we kept playing may have been simply because it was too much fun and stopping abruptly seemed potentially more dangerous than continuing on. Ideally we would have played a slow reggae song to mellow the crowd and ease the revellers slowly homeward. In reality we squeezed in a couple more ska punk songs, ending, I believe, with one called "Punk Dads," during which the edge of the stage resembled an Olympic diving tower during training season. Then they pulled the plug.

The fact that the beer ran out at about the same time that the live music stopped didn't help to smooth things over with the crowd. Angela Mellor, who had waitressed earlier in the afternoon with Catou, and her husband Mel remembered how the mood began to turn rather dark. It was barely midnight and people were ready to party for many more hours. "It seemed that Dusty's was going to get an early demolition," Angela recalled. Some people started picking up chairs and throwing them at the windows. An all-out brawl appeared imminent. Mel attempted to hold the hooligans in check while the evening's MC, Guitar Doug (a.k.a. Daddy-O of the Patio) was given a live mike and began a valiant attempt at calmly talking everybody home.

The Hounds of Buskerville made their way back to Dusty's Den and waited for things to calm down. Our stab at rock stardom nearly complete, there was nothing left to do but drink the only remaining liquor in the fridge and consume illicit substances in the bathroom. When the manager finally showed up the bar was virtually empty except for a few staff members. As it turned out, we weren't only the last band ever to play in the bar, but also the last patrons ever to be thrown out. The good favour we'd held with Dusty's management had clearly expired.

The building remained standing for the demolition crew to begin work the following week. Dusty's management faced a number of liquor licence infractions that resulted in temporary suspensions of their licence over the next few years. While two violations were apparently the most ever handed out in one evening up to that point in the province, Dusty's Last Stand managed to rack up seven. The party lives on indeed.

4

HOPE YOU LIKE JAMMIN' TOO

Whistler has always had a vibrant live music scene. The young people who arrive in town every fall with a pair of skis or a snowboard are almost as likely to be toting a guitar, a notebook with song lyrics or—most recently—two turntables and a microphone. Jam sessions in town have never been short of eager musicians, and new bands form as readily as the snow flies in December. It's a tradition that goes back a long way, as evidenced by a *circa*-1932 black-and-white photo in one of Whistler's history books of the Woods family band with their guitars, fiddles and accordion. While their dad worked for the Pacific Great Eastern Railway, the kids and their mom played summer dances, earning two bucks a piece. Not bad for the dirty thirties.

The guitar I got for Christmas the first winter we lived in Whistler kept me busy for many years. Our one-and-a-half channels of snowy television reception left me with lots of time for sitting around and slowly learning to play the thing. And there

Charlie Doyle, Robin Blechman and Norman Berglund of Skunk Cabbage Review regularly brought their homegrown "folk punk" to the Christianna Inn. PHOTO TIM SMITH

were always role models around town to give me the somewhat mistaken impression that playing music was a respectable and viable way to earn a living. Charlie Doyle, publisher of the *Whistler Answer*, and his girlfriend Robin Blechman performed under the name Skunk Cabbage Review and could often be seen promoting the latest issue while belting out tunes by the Stones and John Hiatt, along with a few original numbers. Doc Fingers, an exceptional piano player and singer with a kind of New Orleans flare, would swing into town on his ski-resort tours and play restaurants and après bars as he still does today. I remember my parents seeing him at The Keg restaurant one night and my dad commenting that he suspected the doctor was high on something, with his faraway glazed expression, but that he sure could play that piano.

Mark Schnaidt

Another musician I would often see playing around town was Mark Schnaidt. Mark played the bass and sang with a mellifluous baritone that stood out in an era of scratchy hip-pie crooners. I can't remember if it was at L'Après or up in Whistler Mountain's Roundhouse where I first heard Mark playing bass in duos or trios in the late seventies. A few years later, he and Charlie Doyle formed a band called Foot in the Door with Rocco Bonito, Craig Barker and a few other revolving members. Having played in bands most of his life, Mark brought a level of professionalism to the group. I stopped by his apartment at the Highland Lodge, a few doors away from the Rimrock Café where he was a cook for many years, to talk about Whistler's early days of live music.

"We rehearsed that band in Craig's basement all summer, twice a week sometimes four or five hours at a time until we had nineteen or twenty songs," Mark said. Foot in the Door quickly started picking up gigs all over the valley. "We were so starved for entertainment, and a bar that had a rock 'n' roll band, everybody in town would go to all of these events. You'd know everybody there, the whole age span from eighteen to fifty at least." The band played National Ski Team benefits at Dusty's, held down Friday and Saturday nights at the Delta Hotel's new Stumps Bar (so named, along with the restaurant Twigs, because the hotel was built on a part of the dump that the excavators discovered was filled with nearly bottomless quantities of dead

After playing bass in a number of Vancouver and Whistler bands, Mark Schnaidt explored his Montana roots by singing and strumming authentic cowboy ballads for the Blackcomb Sleigh Rides. PHOTO ELWYN ROWLANDS

tree matter) and opened the Mountain House, another new bar in the village. I remember hearing them play outside in the village the summer it opened and in the school field after the Great Snow Earth Water Race on the May 24 long week-end. "Flip Flop and Fly," "Take Me To the River" and Charlie's homegrown hit "Skunk Cabbage" ("It don't smell so bad . . .") got people dancing and suited the beer-garden venue perfectly.

The new crop of jammers who arrive in town every fall likely don't realize that they're part of a musical continuum in the valley. As much as Whistler remakes itself each year, when it comes to music and other forms of culture a continuous thread can usually be traced through the decades and I've always seen Mark Schnaidt as a key strand in that thread. Growing up in Kalispell, Montana, near the Canadian border, Mark came by his musical passion honestly. "My dad was a singer in New York City, and when mom got pregnant they decided to move out west," he told me. "He sang German *lieder*, serious music. Richard Strauss was his specialty. He ended up making his liv-ing, just like me, working in the bars, singing high Jewish holi-days and singing in the tabernacles and things like that."

There was lots of music in the Schnaidt family home. Mark's dad taught him some things about breath control in singing, even though the pop music Mark was interested in was an entirely different discipline from the classical music his dad sang. He also told him that show business was a horrible life and to stay as far away from it as possible. Naturally, Mark gravitated straight toward it. "I was bucking bales of hay for fifty cents an hour at the 4-H farm," he said, "and a bale of hay weighs about seventy-five, eighty pounds. You work out there eight hours a day for what, four dollars? The first gig I ever did was at the National Guard Armory when I was a sophomore in high school, and I came home with forty-two dollars for three hours of work." With the proceeds he earned, Mark went out and bought himself a Gibson acoustic guitar that he still plays to this day.

It was 1964, the year the Beatles came to America, and Mark soon became part of a local band called Gang Grein. "It was the era of regional bands," Mark said, "and the big bands in those days were out of Seattle, the Sonics and the Wailers. So we did all of their material and the Kingsmen of course, 'Louie Louie' and 'David's Mood.' In those days most of the bands were instrumentals, but because we had three singers in our band we were a little different, we could actually do the Beatles songs." While Beatlemania swept the nation, Gang Grein was building up its career in the Montana music scene. They designed their own posters, wrote radio spots and rented civic centres in Bute and Helena sometimes a year in advance for state basketball tournament gigs, at times taking home $2500 a night, minus a few expenses. Driving home from one of those gigs in Bute in the guitar player's 1949 Chevy coupe with a U-Haul full of gear, they were held up and robbed at gunpoint at the Anaconda and Bute junction, an unfortunate marker of success for any regional band.

The guitar player and leader of Gang Grein was Troy Evans, now famous for his role as Frank on the TV series *ER*. In 1967, the year Mark graduated from high school, Troy, smooth talker that he was, landed the band a gig at Galena Street East in Aspen working for Don Fleischer, who was promoting the Byrds at the time. If Gang Grein did well, they'd go on tour as an opening act for the Byrds that summer. "This was fantastic," Mark said. "The first night we walked in, the band that we were replacing was playing, an eight-piece band called the Kansas City Soul Association. They had a four-piece horn section, four terrific singers and a four-piece rhythm section. It was phenomenal, they had all the steps, they dressed in slick clothes and were doing all the Sam and Dave tunes and everything spot on, and it was just scary. We walked in and went, 'Wow, what are we doing here?'" In comparison Gang Grein was basically a skilled basement band doing Kingsmen and Spencer Davis Group covers, livened up with some tambourine.

Nonetheless, they took the stage the next night and confidently played their songs. During the first set the club slowly emptied out. Same thing happened the second night. On the third night Don Fleischer showed up after the first set and fired them on the spot. "He paid us for the first two nights because he'd given us a condo up on the hill, and that would pay for our room. But we didn't even have enough money to get gasoline," Mark recalled.

With their tails between their legs and realizing that they were well out of their league at the ritzy Galena Street East, Gang Grein managed to limp into Boulder, Colorado. They got a gig at what was known as a three-two club and found a cheap room on campus. Three-two clubs served 3.2 percent beer, which could be consumed by eighteen-year-olds in Colorado— one of the reasons the under-twenty-one band members were so keen on touring in Colorado. They were back in their element and earning some money, but they had learned an important lesson. Not only could Troy talk them into almost any gig, he was also the band's weakest link with his questionable guitar playing and singing and his beer-infused stage antics. "We decided when we get back we'll have to put the band back together with another guitar player and a better singer. We had to do these Beatles songs better, it was too rough, we had to do more than grow our hair long," said Mark. Despite the fact that Troy started the band, ran it with his brother and owned the '49 Chevy that got them to gigs, they fired him while they were still in Boulder. Troy took it surprisingly well, Mark remembered, until the band got back to Kalispell. Mark managed to get out of the car with his bass guitar, but all the rest of the band's gear stayed in the U-Haul and was promptly locked in Troy's basement. It took a lawyer and a lawsuit to get it back.

The new guitar player was Ronnie McLaren from Lethbridge, Alberta, who became Mark's eventual connection to Canada. Gang Grein evolved into Meridian Road, an eight-member R & B outfit that included a four-piece horn section. Now based in Missoula, Mark was attending university with the rest of his bandmates, taking general arts courses and majoring in a program he referred to as "staying out of Vietnam." Meridian Road played lots of gigs on the university campus and opened up for all the greats who travelled through, including B.B. King, B.J. Thomas and Kenny Rogers in his rock 'n' roll days. When Chuck Berry arrived in town with only a piano player and needed a backup band, Meridian Road was it. "He didn't have any rehearsals—it was crazy," Mark recalled. "He walks in ten minutes before we were supposed to play our first set and says, 'You guys know how to play blues?' We said, 'Yeah, we know the form.' And he says, 'Who's the bass player? I don't want nothing fancy. I want quarter notes on the root, that's all I want to hear out of you.' That was it. That was our rehearsal, and we went out on stage. Fortunately all of his songs are the same. He's got . . ." Mark sang the riff from "Johnny Be Good," then "Oh Carol" and another tune. "He's got three styles. It worked but it was scary."

Playing music two nights a week around Montana, Mark paid for all of his university expenses and managed to keep from being drafted into the military. When Ronnie graduated from university in 1971 he moved to Vancouver with his old bandmates from Lethbridge and Mark went along with them. They shared a house in Port Coquitlam, practised in the basement and, while two of them taught at a music conservatory in Burnaby, they all enjoyed the benefits of Ronnie's wife's good job, which covered many of the bills. Ronnie's band, called Sequoia, hired Barry Samuels as a manager and he had them opening for B.B. King at the Queen Elizabeth Theatre in Vancouver within a few months.

Mark made his move to Whistler after a couple of years playing with Sequoia, but not before an ill-fated trip to Whitehorse, Yukon. Together with his new partner, Lisa Mianscum, and her young daughter Tanya, Mark and two other players took on a seven-night-a-week gig up north. "It was so cold outside, when it got up to twenty below it seemed like it was really warm," Mark recalled. "It was twenty-four-hour darkness, sweating like a pig and then walking out into thirty below weather because we had to walk outside to get from the bar to the hotel." After three months, Mark came down with the worst flu he'd ever had, tinnitus that had him hearing non-stop symphonies in his head, and pneumonia. He and his family finally headed back home to Kalispell, where Mark could take some time to recover before returning to Vancouver.

Disheartened by the music business after his Whitehorse experience, Mark decided to get a real job and attended cooking school for a year. But somehow every time the school gave him a restaurant placement for a practicum, he'd find a better-paying music gig and quit the cooking job. It was the old "humpin' hay bales versus well-paid gig" scenario playing itself out again. Mark finally made up his mind that the only way to finish his cooking practicum was to get out of the city. He had become a regular skier at Whistler, racking up nearly thirty days the previous year, and he'd also played some gigs at the Christianna Inn. Moving to the ski town would cut down on a lot of driving, so when Jack Bright offered him a job cooking at the recently opened JB's in Creekside, he accepted.

Mark completed his practicum under Rolf Gunther, long-time co-owner and chef of the Rimrock Café. The little bar at JB's, presided over by Whistler photographer Greg Griffith, brought in occasional live music and Mark kept his bass there to sit in with whoever was playing. The regulars included Doc Fingers, Joe Conroy and a comic musical duo known as Nails and Lashes. Donny Nails (a.k.a. Donny Cook) was a member of Mark's band Sequoia. He partnered with Lee (Morin) Lashes, who'd gone to Whitehorse with Mark. Lee was quick on his feet with the comedic repartee, but Donny was just crazy, Mark remembered. As part of the act he would dive off the piano straight onto the floor. "He was really into kung fu and kara-te and weightlifting, a real pure guy, you know. No drugs for Donny other than lots of coffee." Donny also had the dubious distinction of breaking his ribs after diving into the pool at JB's. He chose the shallow end, but there happened to be no water in it. Perhaps Mark's dad had a point when he cautioned Mark to stay as far away from show business as possible.

We're Jammin'

My musical path crossed Mark's in the late eighties and early nineties. Jordan White, from the band She Stole My Beer, and some other cooks at the small bistro Citta' began hosting an open jam session in its upstairs room. It was a rough and tum-ble affair that gave emerging players like my brother and me a chance to play in front of a captive audience of unsuspect-ing beer drinkers. Not long after the Citta' jam started, Mark and Charlie decided to resurrect part of Foot in the Door and host a jam at the Boot Pub. Under the moniker of Chequered Past, they enlisted Jordan White with his Hammond B3 organ, local builder and musician Tom McCoy on lead guitar and Lonnie Powell of Headpins fame on drums. After a few suc-cessful jams, they arrived one Wednesday night to find that the Boot had run out of beer as a result of the previous night's Halloween party. The band held the jam anyway, without beer or payment, but moved it the next week to the Longhorn Pub in the village, where it became the hub of Whistler's music scene for the next two years.

All of the musicians who'd played at Citta' and the Boot jams began showing up at the Longhorn on Wednesday nights. They included Guitar Doug Craig, Mike Vollmer, Wendy Wong and Trenton "Trout" Dye, Leanne Lamoureux, Gord Rutherford, Greg Eymondson, Whistler's honorary town busker Franco, Mushroom Mark, Sue Kirkwood, Ian and Rob Boyd, my brother Peter and me and many others. Playing in the dimly lit Citta' was a good way to get your feet wet, but taking the stage at the Longhorn required a whole other level of courage. The pub had a real stage with a good-sized dance floor and a barroom that stretched out and around the corner and could hold 250 people. I remember the feeling of terror the first few times I took the stage and how, if all went well, that feeling would gradually transform into a thrilling high. If you could muster up at least a stab at confidence and professionalism, the solid backing band could accomplish much of the rest.

Dave Branigan, manager of the Longhorn Pub through much of the nineties, had a good eye and ear for live music and regularly brought in bigger touring acts such as Ashley MacIsaac, Fishbone and the Wailers. He also recognized the value of filling his pub every Wednesday night with local musicians and their thirsty friends. Mark remembered that Jack Lavin, host of the long-standing Yale Pub blues jams in Vancouver and co-founder of the Powder Blues Band with his brother Tom, was in one night having a beer with some musician friends. "They all got up and played," Mark recalled, "and Branigan said, 'That's a pretty good idea. We'll get a blues bus going with the Yale players.' They started bringing up a couple of players every week." Having Dave Woodward of the Powder Blues Band sit in on saxophone or Jack Lavin on bass notched up the musical offering and helped draw a bigger crowd.

The musical incubator at the Longhorn encouraged many local Whistler bands to emerge over the next few years, including the Harpoons (with Lumpy Doug and Johnny Thrash of *Ski Bums* movie fame), the Unorthodox Bohemians, Azul, the Wild Dogs of Wedgemount and many others whose names I've forgotten. My brother and I started a band that eventually became known as Route 99. We were both spending a lot of time in Vancouver and we began busking on Granville Island and Robson Street with a friend who played guitar and accordion. The high-fashion district of Robson Street was particularly good for earning us enough loonies to pay for dinner and beer at the Spanish tapas bar La Bodega on Howe Street afterwards. The busking led to indoor gigs and to busking adventures down the Oregon Coast, where we earned enough to keep us going on food, beer and gasoline. Realizing that replicating other band's songs wasn't our strength, we focused instead on originality, playing our own strange blend of Pacific-marinated folk punk.

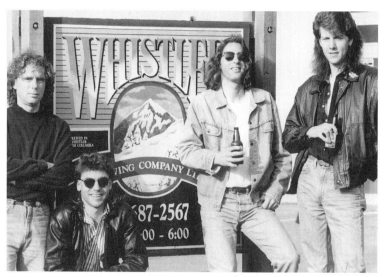

Route 99 members Cam Salay, Peter Vogler, Stephen Vogler and Todd Vague never strayed far from the Whistler Brewing Company while gigging in the valley in the early 1990s. PHOTO ELWYN ROWLANDS

Whistler Village is a potential land of milk and honey for the busker—a pedestrian village full of holiday revellers looking for entertainment and somewhere to spend their money. There's only one problem: the no soliciting bylaw with its maximum $2000 fine. Incidentally, swearing or urinating (in public that is) can land you in the same predicament. Having grown up in this fair valley, however, Peter and I felt it our local right and duty to bring music to the denizens of the village and to challenge such a philistine bylaw. The result was a game of cat and mouse with Whistler's newly uniformed bylaw enforcement officers. At the helm of the organization was Calvin Logue, one of the brothers I'd worked with on the Singing Pass hiking trail. We would set up in clandestine spots, play a few songs and earn a few dollars, all the while keeping a watchful eye out for bylaw enforcement. Fortunately, their recent request to carry billy clubs had been denied (no joke). When rogue buskers encounter the law, they must quickly kick their music cases closed and assume the guise of free-entertainment providers. This ploy worked for a time, but did nothing to smooth over relations with the bylaw department. It got so ridiculous that while busking on the trail between Whistler Village and Blackcomb base, the officers would hide in the surrounding trees and try to catch us on video accepting coins. (I like to think that our persistence helped break trail for the slightly more permissive attitude toward busking in the village now. While the bylaw still exists it is no longer enforced with such zealotry. Franco has been holding down his post on Village Stroll for many years, and just the other day I saw the RCMP walk right past him without saying a word, and even the mayor recently admitted to being a walk-by contributor.)

Fortunately, our persistence in Village Square led to an offer to busk legally on the Citta' patio. From there we worked our way into gigs upstairs. Cam Salay, who later became a member of the Paperboys, had joined us on bass and banjo by this time, and we found ourselves a drummer one night at Citta'. Up to that point we each occasionally took up residence behind a bass drum, snare and hi-hat. When a real drummer by the name of Todd Vague got up out of the crowd and joined us for a few songs, we realized what we'd been missing. During an impressive little solo we looked back and noticed that he was playing with one hand while holding a beer in the other. Of course, we hired him on the spot. Although the band began to gravitate more toward R & B and blues–rock, we still played some East Coast-influenced songs, as our accordion player, Richard Day, had spent time in Newfoundland. During these numbers the serving staff would arm the entire bar with pairs of spoons for an en masse percussion accompaniment.

When Chequered Past ended its regular Wednesday nights at the Longhorn, Route 99 began to host a Sunday night jam at the Boot Pub. All the usual suspects came out to play, and

Brothers Peter and Stephen Vogler fronted the Hounds of Buskerville through many Monday Night Madness gigs at the Boot Pub in the late 1990s. PHOTO CHRIS WOODALL

the local music scene continued to ferment. Cam's brother Joe Salay brought his searing guitar playing to Route 99 and the band played so many gigs in town it sometimes felt as though we were on the road. With so many bars, après patios and parties, Whistler is like that for its musicians. Today the same scene continues with Kostaman and the Vibrations hosting jams at Black's Pub and the Crystal Lounge and with a host of excellent local musicians including Sean Rose, Rob Funk and Rajan Das. "Guitar" Doug Craig and "Grateful" Greg Reamsbottom of the Hairfarmers have turned après patio entertainment into a fine art, playing over 250 gigs a year, while "Creekside" Phil Richard and A Whole Lotta Led sound exactly like Led Zeppelin without trying to look like them.

When the members of Route 99 went their separate ways, my brother and I started the Hounds of Buskerville with a drummer and horn players from Vancouver. We played plenty of gigs in Whistler and Vancouver, toured around BC and the Gulf Islands and went clear across to Saskatoon. The high point of one Western Canadian tour was opening for Men at Work in Calgary and Edmonton. The low point was the night my brother broke his foot on stage at the Rose and Crown in Calgary and had to play the rest of the gig with his foot in traction on a bar stool. Dusty's Last Stand was also, of course, a high point. But whatever happened to Mark Schnaidt?

The Strawberry Roan

Mark continued to play occasional gigs around town and cook fine meals at the Rimrock Café with Rolf Gunther and the rest of the staff, who have stayed like a family with that establishment for a quarter of a century. Early in the new millennium I heard that some horrible luck had befallen Mark. Walking across the highway next to the Whistler Creek Lodge to visit his daughter, Tanya, he got hit by a car. The impact knocked him up in the air and he came down on his head. The humerus in his right arm was pulverized into what Mark's doctor described as crushed corn flakes and his eye was temporarily knocked out of his badly banged up head, which took 127 stitches to patch back together. After hearing of the accident and that Mark was recovering well, the first thought that entered my mind was whether he'd be able to play the bass again. The doctors had to wait months before they could put a plate in his arm, and then the recovery was slow. "Eventually," Mark said, "I started strumming my guitar a lot to see if I could do it. I was using the guitar as therapy."

After two years of rehabilitating his arm, Mark saw an ad in the paper for a gig that could draw on both his Montana roots and his musical skills. An outfit was running horse-drawn sleigh rides from Base Two at Blackcomb to a little cabin in the woods above Lost Lake. They wanted live music with a Western theme to entertain the guests while they sipped their hot chocolate. "I didn't want to sing country music; it probably would have worked fine, but I find that it's not very interesting for me, and so I just learned all these old cowboy songs," Mark said. His dad gave him a songbook he'd had since he was a boy in North Dakota, full of old cowboy songs collected by early ballad hunter Jack Thorp. "Jack Thorp was the guy that went out and saved all this cowboy music; this is sort of like the bible of western music. That's all the cowboy songs ever written right there. I just took those songs and learned them as best I could, and then got some more current recordings so I could get some melodies that were a little more accessible, a little more melodic."

Most of the tunes are straightforward and simple, Mark said, Celtic melodies from old Irish and Scottish folk songs, popular songs of the day when Stephen Foster was writing hits. But it was the lyrics that really captivated him. "They're all old stories about various cattle rustlers, bank robbers, cowboy heroes that rode this horse or that. A lot of them are about horses that couldn't be ridden, or rode, as they say. I quite enjoyed it because they're all kind of epic poems, you know. Twenty-two verses in some of them, so it takes forever to memorize it." Other songs feature historic characters, including "The Ballad of Jesse James" and one about the legendary bandit Sam Bass.

To record the lyrics of these songs, Jack Thorp lived the cowboy life and went along on western trail drives. "There were a couple of trails—the Chisholm Trail was one of them that started in Texas and went up to Omaha, I think," said Mark. "They would drive the cattle up to the railheads and that only went on for a few decades, after the Civil War and until the turn of the century, and then the cowboys were gone. But there was a real oral tradition with all these cowboys, and our romantic version of the West is from those two decades, the 1870s and 1880s. Our impression of the cowboy and the Wild West is all from this little snapshot in time, and these are the stories that really happened at the time."

Mark continued adding these songs to his repertoire as he played for the sleigh ride guests. The horses would pull them along an old logging road on Blackcomb Mountain to a ramshackle cabin in the woods that was really nothing more than a glorified tent. There was no electricity, so the place was lit by about a dozen kerosene lamps. Each of the two sleighs carried about fourteen people, a few more if there were lots of kids. Twenty-five to thirty people would huddle in the tent on old blanket-covered couches with their hot chocolates and listen to the cowboy music. A more authentic western experience was never delivered in Whistler. I can almost hear the ghost of Dusty whinnying appreciatively.

Mark played four twenty-minute sets seven evenings a week, adding an extra set on holidays. The gig lasted for six winters and was one of the most solid and best-paying of his musical career. "I really enjoyed it," he told me. "It broke my heart when that cabin burned down. That was the end of it. They couldn't build anything up there that they could insure because it was on Crown land." A lot of locals also made it up on the sleigh rides to hear Mark sing his cowboy ballads. I unfortunately never did get there, but I asked Mark at the end of our talk if he'd play one of the songs for me. He took out his Martin guitar and played one of his favourites, "The Strawberry Roan." As Mark strummed the guitar in three-quarter time and sang the cowboy lyric with a lilt in his voice, I was transported up to the cabin on Blackcomb Mountain, and from there all the way back to Montana and down the Chisholm Trail of the 1870s:

> I was laying around just spending my time
> Out of a job I ain't got a dime
> Out steps a feller and says I suppose
> You're a bronc fighter by the look of your clothes
> I said I'm a good one, a good one I claim
> Do you happen to have any bad ones to tame
> He said I've got one, a bad one to buck
> For throwing good riders he's had lots of luck
>
> He said this old pony has never been rode
> The boy that gets on him is bound to get throwed

It occurred to me by the second verse that Mark had truly earned the right to play these old cowboy songs. I don't know if he ever rode a strawberry roan, but he *was* thrown high in the air by a black Audi on Highway 99.

5

Up the Mountain

Mogul Skiing, or My Misspent Youth

If Whistler has its own version of broncobusting, it would be
mogul skiing. When I began my career as a mogul skier, the
discipline—and I use that term loosely— was still far from an
Olympic sport. I remember hearing about the training regi-
men of ski racers. They worked on slalom technique with their
coaches on the mountain, did dryland and weight training in
the off-season as well as something called stretching. Not so for
the mogul skier. There was no local freestyle or mogul coach in
the late seventies. Training involved getting up the mountain
whenever possible: weekends, holidays and those slow periods
at school that often coincided with a new snowfall.

I would ride up the long, often-wet Olive Chair, then the
slow, freezing and windblown Red. Once at the top if I was too
frozen to ski, I'd pop into the Roundhouse to throw my gloves
and jacket on a heater or into the dryer downstairs. The juke-
box was always pumping out Steve Miller's "Space Cowboy"
or Creedence Clearwater Revival's "Sweet Hitchhiker," and the
local ski bums sat rolling joints and then lighting them up in

the blue-green haze. As a young teenager and relatively new local, I recall staring wide-eyed at this strange ritual with the illicit green herb. To my new friends in town, some of whose parents were squatters and ski bums themselves, it was all perfectly natural. Sometimes the ski bums at the next table *were* their parents.

With warm gloves and a contact high, I'd head out to Chunky's Choice. Chunky's was the perfect training ground for the aspiring mogul skier. From the relatively short twelve-minute ride on the Blue Chair you could see who else was out that day and easily connect with your friends. It was a veritable terrain park before such a thing existed. On a typical Saturday morning I might have come across the likes of Steve, Geoff and Holly Morrison, Janet and Richard Angus, Brian and Richard Van Stratten, Matt Bolton, Robbie Thibeault, Kelley Corbin,

Look Ma, no toe pieces!" The author pops a 360 off a jump on the Ridge Run, *circa* 1976. PHOTO COURTESY THE AUTHOR

Don McGregor, Vicky and Peter Vogler, John Smart, Peggy Meyers, Ray Mason, Rumi Merali, and the list could go on.

On a good day, a serious bumper could get twenty to twenty-five runs in on Chunky's. The first pitch offered a few good turns then a swing to the right. The next was much longer but became more shallow in the middle, offering good opportunities for air: instead of sucking up the bumps and keeping your skis on the snow, you could launch off one of them and throw a spread eagle, a twister-spread, daffy, or if you were feeling particularly on your game that day, a 360.

The last pitch was where you could really show your stuff. It was on view not only by the riders on the lower part of the chair but also by the entire lift line. The pitch was steep and demanding and had a little ledge at the bottom where you could take some big air. On quiet days, the Blue Chair liftees would also keep an eye on the last face of Chunky's. One of them was a guy named Ken Melamed who later became Whistler's Olympic mayor. Ken would often make amiable comments such as "Nice run," or "Good turns," or sometimes the more cryptic "Sustainability is key," with a faraway look in his eye, as though he could see into the future.

When you stand at the top of a mogul pitch, you size up the bumps and begin to pick your line. You need only pick it a few moguls ahead, because stuff will happen between now and then that you can't foresee, and you want to keep your options open. The mogul skier uses the same quick carves as the slalom skier. Edge to edge, hands in front, still upper body facing downhill, legs pumping up and down like pistons, skis sucking onto the snow like a vacuum cleaner. It's rodeo with the busting bronc replaced by Volkswagen-sized bumps on a healthy diet of gravity. Now, take that account and speed it up until the West Coast flakes are flying past your face in a frozen blur and your knees are pumping as fast as the pistons in a four-cylinder

car heading to the Creekside on Saturday morning. Keep looking ahead, always looking ahead. Mogul skiing is about surviv-
ing with style and there's no room for superfluous movements.
The mogul skier doesn't wiggle his bum.

And speaking of style, in 1977 I wore bright red Dynafit
ski boots and yellow Head Yahoo skis. My suit was a brilliant
red one-piece with a dash of orange and yellow at the pock-
ets. I used to be somewhat embarrassed by these details of my
teenage ski years; now I dig them up with the relish of a ski
archeologist. Everything was red, orange and yellow in the mid-
seventies. Lange boots came in every shade of those colours. I
remember the ski magazine ad with the sexy blond stretched
across two pages, her hand draped suggestively over a Lange
boot: "Soft Inside," the caption read. I thought it referred to the
ski boots.

While Whistler didn't have a freestyle club or a coach in the
seventies, Jim McConkey's Ski School did offer mogul clinics.
One of the instructors offering these bump clinics was John
Colpitts, who had a later career as a L'Après DJ and boot-fitter.
John already had an extravagant knee brace holding his leg
together—perhaps not a great selling point for the aspiring
bumper—but he was a good mogul skier who taught the proper carved turn as opposed to the slap-bang windshield-wiper
technique favoured by some mogul practitioners—those who
tended to end up shorter at the end of the season than they'd
started out in November.

I did well in my first mogul contest on Chunky's Choice—
the home snow advantage didn't hurt—and John offered to
take me to the BC Freestyle Championships at Silver Star that
spring. He showed up at the drive in front of the Tyrol Lodge in
a blue Chevy Nova along with a friend named Brent Kirkpatrick
who would be entering the men's senior category. My parents
must have had a strong sense of trust in their newly adopted

community, because they had no qualms about sending me off across the province in the back of a Chevy Nova with a couple of ski bums in their early twenties. It was somewhere along the Hope–Princeton Highway that John and Brent rolled up the first hash spliff and offered it to me. I declined. Not only was I a serious athlete now, but I was still a little jumpy on mountain highways.

This trip took place not too long after our family's fateful slide off the edge of Highway 99 toward the Cheakamus Canyon. I'd been asleep in the back seat as the car had left the road and, as testimony to my devotion to mogul skiing, the bumping, bouncing motion had me dreaming that I was skiing some car-sized moguls. As I rose a little higher toward wakefulness, I realized that I was *in* a car and that it had probably gone off the road. Ever the optimist, I pictured the ditch on the right side, a nice, ten-foot drop to a relatively safe stop. The car, my brother and dad later told me, was actually starting to roll onto its side, ready to go over, when it hit the one small tree that stopped us and set the Oldsmobile back on its wheels.

In a cloud of hashish and tobacco smoke, John and Brent and I made it safely to Vernon and pulled up at the house of BC Freestyle Team coach Steve Hubbard. Steve was a short, friendly, rather gnomish character who was a mentor to the team, both in skiing and partying. They set me up in a room and headed off to the Village Green Pub for some late-night fun. I recall waking in the morning to the strains of Bob Dylan's "Stuck Inside of Mobile with the Memphis Blues Again" and the giggly laughter of a couple of young women who'd accompanied John and Brent home from the Village Green. At fourteen, it appeared I had a lot to look forward to.

We skied Silver Star the next day, then moved to the Village Green Hotel where I met some of the other competitors, people I'd get to know better over the next four or five years of freestyle competitions. The cast of characters included Brett Wood, Al and Neil Bidell, Al McGregor and Nadine Nesbitt from the Kootenays, Brad Suey and Peter Wagner from Prince George, Sue Boyd from Tillicum Valley, Tom Simister, Dave Wallin and Davianna Young from Whistler, Doug Schwary and Keith Reid from Vancouver and on and on. Oddly, I don't remember much about the mogul competition itself, except that the bumps were big, with a bit of loose Okanagan powder on top, the sun came out and the run wasn't as steep as Chunky's Choice. Brent and I both finished in the top three of our respective categories. My mogul career was launched.

John and Brent decided to carry on to some other ski areas in the Interior, but they arranged a ride home for me with Ray Mason. Ray was a great mogul skier. He kept his hands tight in front of him and skied smooth and really fast. He drove the same way, all the way through Hell's Gate and the rest of the Fraser Canyon down to Hope and Vancouver and back up to Whistler. When I stepped up to the front door of our house, my BC Championships medal tucked into my backpack, I felt as though I'd just survived a great adventure, in style—which is what mogul skiing is all about.

The Sextathlon

Over my five years of participating in freestyle competitions, I recall Brett Wood at almost every one of them. Whether it was the Shell Cup Nationals at Mount Norquay in 1978, the BC Championships at Big White in 1979 or pro dual mogul contests in the States in the early eighties, you could count on Brett being there. And while I left competitive skiing around the time I finished high school, Brett kept following the mogul tour, joined the Barnum and Bailey Circus with a ski aerialist show and eventually became an aerials coach with the BC Freestyle Team. But of all the ski competitions Brett entered over the years, the one he speaks of with the most relish took place on home turf on Blackcomb Mountain. Shortly after the event, Brett described it in a local journal, *The Rolling Whistler Review,* as "more fun than a gondola full of ganja." What set the Sextathlon apart from any other ski competition was that it took six different ski disciplines and rolled them all into one great, unsanctioned, two-day event, attracting Whistler's best skiers from a broad variety of backgrounds. Mogul skiers had to prove their mettle in the gates, racers had to show that they could handle a steep, icy mogul pitch and everybody had to test their courage off the huge, floating gelande jump, until the best overall skier emerged.

I'd sadly missed the event due either to travelling or study-ing in the mid-eighties, so Brett kindly recreated it for me over a drink at Roland's Pub in the Creekside. "I believe it was Hugh O'Reilly's brainchild. He was on the Blackcomb ski patrol at the time," Brett told me. "It was his, let's call it his last act of defiance," he said. (O'Reilly later became a three-term mayor of Whistler.) "It was an underground event, and once man-agement got wind of it, they actually showed up and saw that it was quite cool and let things continue. I'm sure that they had second thoughts during the gelande event." Entrants had to use one pair of skis for all six disciplines, and broken skis could only be replaced by the same length and type of ski—a factor that came into play in dramatic fashion throughout the weekend.

The first event was a dual slalom with pro jumps, mak-ing use of the intact course from the previous weekend's PWA pro slalom race. As a mogul skier, Brett held his own among local racers, including Tom Charron, Ricky Lewon and Jordan Williams, and placed a respectable fifth. The gate skiers were still in the driver's seat after the super giant slalom, won by Ricky Lewon. Then came the mogul event. "Being the resident mogul mutt, Hugh O'Reilly let me choose the mogul run, so I chose the last pitch of Staircase, a run I knew I would do well on and all the racers would cry over," Brett said, taking a pull from his eponymous tequila, Grand Marnier and lime juice over ice, known in these parts as a Woody. "Ricky Lewon made about four turns and went straight into the bush. Tommy Charron hit the ski patrol snowmobile at the bottom and broke his skis, first of two pairs that day I believe. The judges just split, they saw him coming and they all ran. Tommy, being of a racing background and from the east, was a little heavy on the edges, not letting those edges go quick enough," Brett added, getting his one-two punch in on both easterners and ski racers. (In his defence, Tom later pointed out to me that he had just returned from a vitamin-infused all-nighter in Vancouver to see the Butt-Hole Surfers, and that it was his intention to be the fastest skier on the course). Brett won the mogul event, followed by his freestyle buddies Brad Suey and Brad Van Couer, who went on to appear in Warren Miller ski films. Scott Elder, who had chewed out Brett for picking a run that "nobody would get down," came in fourth.

The *gelandesprung* is a time-honoured competition originating in Europe where skiers with regular alpine equipment see how far they can launch themselves off a large jump with a fast in-run. After having won the Super G race, Ricky Lewon took top spot in the gelande as well, though not without controversy. "Ricky was the only guy to win two events; in one of them he cheated," Brett maintained. "But great for Ricky, he really impressed the crowd. However, everybody else was obeying the proper protocol for gelande jumping, which was never going above the in-run ceiling. Because you only got three jumps, the stick never got up to where Ricky was starting from, but we were all catching him, all the guys playing by the rules. He went 214 feet, Jordan Williams went 175, Scott Elder went 146,

I went 145, and you can look that up, those are accurate stats." It should be noted that Brett's memory for statistics can be considered accurate to within 1 percent, twenty times out of twenty. It should also be noted that the only girl to enter the Sextathlon, Rimrock Café waitress and sporty hip gal Sue Clark, beat some of the guys in the gelande contest.

Big mountain free skiing has become a prominent feature of competitive skiing over the past two decades, but Blackcomb's 1987 Sextathlon may well have hosted the world's first free-skiing competition. Saudan Couloir, now called Couloir Extreme, was the site of the free-skiing event in which local Québécois daredevil Phillip Lavoie showed himself to be as innovative as the event itself. "It was basically from the top of Saudan to the bottleneck where it breaks wide open. That little funnel was the finish line," Brett recalled. "Everybody else skied out in the open pitch and tried to impress the judges with their technical skills. Phil actually did the run the way today's competitive big-mountain free skier would have done it. He picked a gnarly line with air. Nobody even thought of that. He basically went out of sight, went skier's left down False Face. I was standing right beside the judges watching uphill—he took two turns, went out of sight and came back into view near the bottom just above the judges, made about five turns and then took about a twenty-five-foot jump right onto the judges, literally, and stopped ten feet from them, for the win."

While Phillip's all-out gutsy innovation wrapped up the free-skiing title, Brett had his own near-Machiavellian plan to capture the final event, an Inferno Race. "In the first days of ski racing, an inferno race was from point A to point B, you picked your own line, and you had to make what they call in a rally, checkpoints. The first checkpoint was Road Runner, which is basically going up the Chimney for the climb to CBC North.

Then it was straight down and the next checkpoint was the trail into the original Overbite, down the bottom pitch of Overbite and then the finish was about where the Glacier Express bull-wheel is now. It was basically a downhill race on an ungroomed run."

Brett reminded me that this was only a few weeks after Canadian downhiller Todd Brooker had barely survived his spectacular rag-doll crash on the Hannenkahm at Kitzbuhel. "There was Ricky Lewon who, when he made his turn on Roadrunner, had a Todd Brooker nightmare himself where he lost all of his equipment, even one of his gloves—both skis, both poles, and a glove was still stuck in one of his pole straps."

As for Brett, everybody told him afterwards that he probably would have won the Inferno if the incident on Overbite hadn't occurred. "I actually went through the trees instead of skiing the trail because I knew the trail would be a whoop-de-do course, and by then I knew my legs would be done and it'd probably be smoother through the trees. When I got to where the main run turns left toward the fall line, there used to be a big slash pile at the top of the run—my strategy had been to come out of the trees, bank and shave speed on the slash pile because it went uphill, and then I was going to go straight down the right side of Overbite because I knew it was smooth."

As it turned out, about a dozen of Brett's friends had parked themselves on the slash pile to watch his creative and potentially winning descent. "Instead of just staying where they were, because they wouldn't have affected me, they ran—they were like ants on a crumb at a picnic, but in reverse, running away from the crumb, the slash pile being the crumb—and so as soon as I saw them all sitting there and starting to move, I adjusted my line. I was still trying to shave speed and I went to go above the slash pile and make a big water-ski turn around it, and get ready for my approach to the last pitch.

"So as I came around the slash pile onto the final pitch, I caught an edge and I ended up on my left ski with my right ski flapping. I went on one ski right into the bottom and the transition ate me up, because by now I was on one leg; on two legs I would have had just enough strength to have survived the transition and made the corner for the dead-flat finish line."

I ordered Brett another Woody so he could finish his harrowing tale. "When I hit the bottom of the compression I took a big rib shot, it knocked the wind out of me. I had decided that was the end of my run. However, the late Lindsay MacIntosh was right there—because there was a group of people standing at the bottom of Overbite figuring that's where the best action would be—when I came crashing into the bottom. I was lying there for easily thirty seconds, totally given up, but I still had one ski on my foot. Lindsay came running up, she started yelling at me, 'Woody! Woody! You got to get up! You wouldn't believe it, you're right in there, right in there!' So I got up, and with one foot poled and kicked my way to the finish line, and was only out of first place by twenty seconds, after just totally giving up and lying there."

That was the kind of commitment the Sextathlon demanded of its entrants. Brett placed a respectable fourth overall out of a field of thirteen. Jordan Williams, ex-Whistler Mountain Ski Club racer and coach, great all-round skier and nice guy, took the Grand Prix title, with Brett's nemesis Ricky Lewon in second place. The after-party was the last of the famous White Parties at the UBC Club Cabin, with live music by Jack Lavin's Chequered Demons. "You brought clear or white liquor for the punch bucket, which was a garbage can," Brett recalled, "and you were supposed to wear white. At that party, Lindsay MacIntosh [known fondly at the time as Chi Chi La Roo] became so obnoxious near the end of the party that she was hoisted by her heels and dunked in the punch bucket to shut her up."

Miraculously, there were no serious injuries from the event, or the after party for that matter, apart from a few sore ribs and bruised shins. The Sextathlon has never been held again, and there are no indications that the International Olympic Committee will be adopting it as an official Olympic sport. But as a means of determining the best overall skier while having more fun than a gondola full of ganja, the Sextathlon remains unmatched.

Off to the Circus

Brett Wood's stint with the Barnum and Bailey Circus can be traced back to a freestyle demonstration held in Prince George in 1986. Brad Suey, who hails from that city and has since been inducted into the Prince George Sports Hall of Fame, organized the event and called up Brett to do the mogul demonstration. But when he saw his old buddy from the Kootenays launch a backflip off the kicker and land near the bottom of the landing hill, he said, "Woodrow, I didn't know you could jump!" Not long afterwards, Brett got a call from a Brett Brown, asking him if he wanted to join the circus. "I was working at Club Ten at the time," said Brett, "and I had reservations about the whole thing because I would have had to leave them, and I was kind of like part of the family by then. But J.J. and Simone [the club owners] said, 'You gotta go for it man, this'll be the chance of a lifetime, think of the life experience.'"

Brett Brown and Paul Gaddick were partners in the Ramp and Tramp Flying Circus and it was their agent, Tim Capp, a trampolinist from New Jersey, who hooked up the gig with Barnum and Bailey. "I hadn't jumped on plastic [sliding surface] for a long time," Brett said, "and I had to go and do some shows to learn how to be a showman." He travelled with the ramp and tramp show that summer and on one of his first jumps in Ottawa, Brett came down on his shoulder and tore his rotator cuff. It was a long, slow recovery, but he could still jump. "I used to climb the scaffold using my chin, like a cocka-too, like a budgie or something on its perch, because my right arm was useless. I couldn't lift it above my shoulder to grab the next rung."

Ski jumpers in indoor shows traditionally landed on a flat inflatable bag, but that all changed in Ottawa. "There were a couple of jumps where Brad Suey landed on the flat bag and skied right off the end of it, and Tim [Capp] said, 'Hey, that ski-ing looks way better than you guys just coming in and going "Bang!" and bouncing up and down a couple of times and walk-ing off.' So he said, 'What if we take that airbag and tilt it?' So me being a carpenter, I built a giant sawhorse at the back of the bag and got a bunch of long two-by-eights set up on the saw-horse to angle the bag. It probably had a twenty-degree slope. And so now we started to ski away, and changed the flatbed ski-jump show into a more dynamic skiing-looking ski show."

From Ottawa it was down to the big leagues in Florida. At the beginning of the Disney animated movie, Dumbo the elephant is born in a barn based on the one in Venice, Florida, where the Barnum and Bailey Circus has trained for over a cen-tury. This is where Brett spent a month rehearsing for his three-ring tour. They not only worked on the act, including two jump-ers descending the four-foot-wide ramp side by side and flip-ping into the airbag, but designed and modified the jump and the landing apparatus. Brett designed and sketched an airbag based on the angled one he pioneered in Ottawa and passed on the specifications to Don, the guy in charge of apparatus devel-opment at Barnum and Bailey. The result was a fully inflatable landing surface—with no more need for two-by-eights—that included a truncated triangular bag underneath and sewn-in berms so that the skiers could bank back to the middle if they veered after landing.

The sliding surface on the jump was covered with a new, untested product called Pro Snow. "We called it 'No Go Pro Slow' because it was so slow," Brett said. "It was like skiing on slush. We spent a week trimming all the bristles shorter to make them stiffer so we'd go faster." The jump itself also required modifications after Brett and Paul Gaddick tested it with their side-by-side double backflip—the feature of the Canadian aerialists' show. "The jump literally fell like a drawbridge from the G forces," Brett remembered. New bracing was installed from the lip of the jump down to the floor in front of the airbag to withstand the forces of the simultaneous jump. The one safety feature that didn't get added was padding on the braces—an omission that came back to bite Brett during a show in Sacramento, California.

When the Greatest Show on Earth embarked on its tour by train across the US, Brett's girlfriend Michelle Bush joined him. Michelle, a colourful Whistler character in her own right who went on to become a local actor, comedian and street performer, had been hired as the nanny for the performance director's three-year-old daughter. When the train chugged out of Venice, it was discovered that Brett and Michelle's stateroom, previously occupied by a breakdancing act, was due for a renovation. Among other problems, the rocking train churned up the sewage tank, making for a smelly journey. Michelle and Brett were given the opportunity to design their own "dream stateroom," all nine-by-fourteen feet of it. "The showgirls," Michelle told me over the phone from her summer B & B on Savary Island, "had eight-by-five feet. 'Almost as big as the tiger cages,' they'd say."

The closest Michelle got to performing in the circus happened late one night after she and Brett and one of the animal trainers had been out clubbing in Philadelphia. Michelle had always wanted to ride an elephant, and perhaps emboldened by the Jack Daniels, she suggested they try it. The trainer, Booker Tyrone Taylor, walked along the cages with them and chose a young African elephant named Mary, "because she's a challenge," he said. Elephants know when they're not on the job, Michelle said, and Mary was shaking her head as if to say "forget it" right from the get-go. Tyrone eventually got Mary to present her knee and lift them up. "As soon as she had us up she started rolling her head," Michelle recalled. "I'm not a rodeo rider so I didn't know what to do. We managed to stay on, then she flicked her shoulder and we just went flying into the air, landing in a heap. My head missed a spike that held one of

Flying Canadian aerialists Paul Geddick (l) and Whistlerite Brett Wood perform rapid-fire double backflips while touring with the Barnum and Bailey Circus in 1989. PHOTO COURTESY BRETT WOOD

her chains." How many people have woken up the next morning with a sore hip and a bit of a hangover and proudly recalled, "Oh yeah, I got thrown from an elephant."

The Flying Canadian aerialists' show was a hit with the Barnum and Bailey Circus. The top of the in-run was in the first ring, and by the time the skiers flipped through the air, landed on the airbag and skied off, they had sailed all the way to the third ring. The farther south they travelled with the show, the more exotic the idea of ski jumpers was to the audience. In Alabama they were such a big hit that famed animal tamer Gunther Gebel-Williams stopped talking to them. As the main attraction of the circus, he didn't like being upstaged by a team of flipping Canadians. Gunther was known as The Boss, Brett said, because he put on three shows, owned and looked after all of his animals and took half of the gate sales. "And his animals were happy," Brett said. "I only have good things to say about Gunther. The bear trainer from Eastern Europe, on the other hand, put muzzles on his bruins and disciplined them with an iron bar. They looked embarrassed to perform."

In New York the circus played Madison Square Garden for two weeks. They were set up right near the New York Rangers' dressing room and Guy Lafleur and Michel Petit were always the first ones in the Garden, Brett recalled. "He'd walk around in his long johns, and the showgirls were asking, 'Who's that guy in the long johns talking to you everyday?' It was incredible. We were hanging out with Guy Lafleur."

Brett's other big city experiences included foiling an attempted robbery in New York City and finding himself in the middle of an armed drug battle in Oakland, California. The circus with three rings also began to heat up. The show evolved and grew as it crossed the country and it became more fun both for the performers and the audience. "In LA the band was starting to play samples of 'O Canada' during the ski-jump act,"

Brett recalled. "Then the spies came out from the east coast and saw that we were having too much fun. The show wasn't exactly as it had been produced by Mr. Kenneth Feld in Venice." By the time they hit Sacramento, the director called a meeting with all the performers. "He was very sombre and serious; I guess his job was on the line or something."

But it wasn't the performance director cracking his whip that sent Brett packing from the circus. The side-by-side double backflip jump was the finale of the Canadian aerialists' show. It required both skiers to lock arms on the in-run so they would leave the lip of the jump at exactly the same time. At the end of one show in Sacramento, Paul Gaddick pushed off a little ahead of Brett, and even the freshly trimmed No Go Pro Slow didn't allow Brett to catch up to his partner. As they got near the lip of the jump, their arms were still locked and Paul took off first. "It was the banana peel effect going off the jump," Brett remembered. "My upper body was sideways, my feet just went right out and I hit the lip of the jump with my upper body, flew through the air, hit the back of the airbag, came back on my head, and I fell backwards. There was this [unpadded] brace between the two struts—both my knees were fully hyper-extended and both my kneecaps were dented."

When an accident happens in the circus, the ring lights instantly go off and the outer track is lit up so the clowns can divert attention away from the cleanup site. Brett managed to stay conscious, but he lay still in case he'd done any damage to his back or neck. He was tied onto a spine board and hauled back into the medical room. "While I was in there, Paul came in and said, 'Woody, is there anything I can get you?' And I said, 'Yeah, Paul, can you get me a pillow for my knees?' They were hurting from the hyperextension because they were laid out flat on the spine board. And one of the medical guys said, 'No, we can't do that, spine, wrong, got to keep you flat.' He was following protocol for lawsuits, because we were in America. But by then I'd realized there was nothing wrong [with his back] because I'd been testing myself."

Brett was still in his performance costume and ski boots when the medics had taped him down across the ankles, knees, hips, shoulders and forehead. "The accident happened on the last jump of the act," he said, "and our act was so high energy because we had to run fifty metres back up to the top of the jump every time. So we were sweating bullets by the end of the show, every time guaranteed." On the way to the hospital, the ambulance attendant kindly asked Brett if there was anything he could get to make him more comfortable. Again, Brett said he'd really like a pillow underneath his knees. "No, we can't do that," the attendant said.

"I'm not going to have to wiggle out of this bad tape job you guys have pulled on me just so I can bend my knees, am I?" Brett asked him, and the attendant jokingly challenged him: "Well, you can try." Brett's ski jumping career may have been on hold due to injury, but he still might have found work in the circus as an escape artist. The tape didn't stick too well on a sweaty Canadian ski jumper, and by the time they pulled up to the hospital, Brett was sitting up on the edge of the stretcher, elbows on his knees, looking out the front window.

"I hadn't said a word and the attendant hadn't looked back. When we got there I said, 'Okay, do you want me to get back on the spine board so you guys look good when you take me in?' And the guy, he freaked! I think he saw his whole life going down the drain because of a lawsuit that was about to happen from this Canadian."

They tied Brett back down and took him into the emergency room where the circus continued. "The attending doctor in Emergency that night was a young guy—good-looking dude— and I swear that every nurse on that night was a Victoria's

Secret model—drop-dead gorgeous, built California girls—and this doctor, he couldn't keep his mind on medicine, he was just too busy making runs at the nurses. And when we came in he was at the nurse's station and it was like, 'Ah shoot, I got to go to work now.' He comes in and they do the X-rays, check me out, everything's fine. By now the doctor's letting me sit up and he says, 'Is there anything else I should check out?' And I go, 'Yeah, my knees.' My knees were never checked. Nobody listened—the doctor was too horny, the ambulance guys were too worried about my spine to listen to the patient. And then I walked out of there. I could have walked off the [circus] floor, but I thought aw, since the clowns are out maybe I'll let the guys come and cart me out."

Shortly after the accident Brett left the Barnum and Bailey Circus and returned to Whistler. "I had to recover anyway, so they let me go home and I never came back."

The Ski Patrol Bomb Shack Museum

Going off to join the circus is one way of making a living in the ski world, but many other people work with boards on their feet right here in Whistler. When my brother-in-law, Ian Bunbury, made his epic journey with Dusty the Horse from Whistler to Blackcomb, he was a rookie ski patroller fulfilling a strange and unsanctioned initiation right. Now, twenty years later, he's a veteran of the force and a valuable member of the Canadian Avalanche Rescue Dog Association with his second avalanche dog, Hector the Protector. Ian recently showed me a fascinating slice of life on the mountain when he took me for a visit to the Ski Patrol Bomb Shack Museum.

"Explosives. Keep Out," reads the sign at the entrance to the bomb shack on Whistler Mountain. Ian instructed Hector to wait out in the blowing snow as we entered the little cabin overlooking Harmony Bowl from the top of GS Run. He

Ski patroller Ian Bunbury and his rescue dog Hector discuss who will drive the snowmobile today. PHOTO TOSHI KAWANO

arrives here early on avalanche control mornings to prepare the charges that will be thrown onto unstable slopes to release potential avalanches. The real reason for our trip lay beneath the floor of the bomb shack, but first Ian gave me a tour of the upstairs where he assembles bombs from ammonium nitrate fuel oil cartridges, blasting caps, fuses and ignitors. "I can wrap 125 of these in an hour," he said.

The igniters are kept free of moisture in a broken-down sticker-covered fridge that was moved here from the ski patrol bump room. It was the first hint of the relics we were about to uncover. Ian lifted a trap door in the floor and we descended a flight of wooden stairs into the past. Snow had drifted in here and there and draped a cold finger into an old Salomon ski boot, a white arm around a historic rescue toboggan. I was reminded of the movie *Margaret's Museum*: some of the old equipment down there wouldn't have been out of place in a Nova Scotia mining town.

"This is a second-generation Tod-boggan, developed at Tod

Mountain," Ian said, suddenly transformed from ski patroller into museum curator. "The early ones were wooden, but this one was built from a new, revolutionary material known as fibreglass," he added, his dry sense of humour never far from the surface. Above the toboggan hangs a bronze ski-school bell with the inscription: "Presented to Whistler Mountain Rock Patrol from Grouse Mountain Snew Patrool [sic] 1978–79." It was donated after a meagre snow year when Vancouver's Grouse Mountain had to close and Whistler invited the Grouse volunteer patrollers up to help out and, more importantly, to ski. Beside the bell is an old black rotary telephone from the Alamo, the liftee shack and central party location that once stood at the bottom of the old T-bar. The first harness to hold a Motorola radio sits beside the phone and hanging on a nail from a beam is Ian's dad Alex "AC" Bunbury's ski patrol fanny pack, retired after thirty years of use on the volunteer patrol.

Then there's the machinery: the first compressed-nitrogen avalanche gun; a steel post with bicycle wheel that was part of

Ian steps through the trap door and into the past at the Ski Patrol Bomb Shack Museum. PHOTO TOSHI KAWANO

a bomb tram to drop charges in inaccessible areas; and a host of lift-evacuation devices. These last items are basically wheels with a brake: the patroller hangs under the wheel while making his way down the lift cable to lower the stranded riders. Each has a harrowing training-session story attached to it to explain why it's bent out of shape or no longer used. A machined piece of aluminum known as a wonder bar and used for lowering people from a gondola looks surprisingly like a smoker's pipe. "It's the only lowering device that can get you higher," Ian said.

And then there are the skis lined up across one wall: Dynastar MV2s from the late sixties; Hart Galaxie II with Marker Simplex DL bindings from 1966; a pair of 1974 Rossignol ROC 550s with Salomon 555 gold springs; Dynamic VR17s; Olin Mark Is with Salomon 502s; an early Lange Comp five-buckle boot; and an even older one made by Koflach. The model names and numbers have significance only to skiers who recall the era. They're all the top performance models, Ian said, what the best skiers were using in the day. "You look at

Strange torture device or another discarded piece of rescue equipment at the Bomb Shack Museum? PHOTO TOSHI KAWANO

this stuff and laugh, but we all used it and it worked well or it wouldn't have been fun."

I consider all the ski cabins in the valley with their own little museums: discarded chair lifts or gondolas in the backyard, skis hanging on the wall and ancient boots on shelves. In a place of such rapid change, perhaps one of the ways we try to understand our existence is by contemplating these discarded artifacts. But the bomb shack museum is more than a mere resting place for old equipment. "It's a living museum where you can actually use the stuff," Ian said. On occasion the exhibits have even been known to travel. "Jason Faulkner and James Retty from the Escape Route just went down to Colorado for *Powder Magazine*'s ski testing," Ian said. "I sent them down with a pair of early-seventies Head HRP Comps and Fischer C4s with Marker Explodomats."

The museum, by the way, might one day be open for guided tours once the explosives are moved to a new storage area.

6

THE PRINT REVOLUTION

The *Whistler Answer*

My good friend Charlie Doyle lives on Easy Street with his partner Mieke Prummel and their now-grown kids, Eryn and Sophie. Their house is next door to Bob and Kashi Daniels and just around the corner from Andy and Bonnie Munster. Reading this, you might get the impression that most of Whistler lives on Easy Street, but that's not quite the case. I, for example, reside just across the tracks on Starving Artist Drive. If I were to identify some of the early influences that landed me in this pleasant, if somewhat downscale neighbourhood, I'd point to Charlie and his creative cohorts at the *Whistler Answer, circa* 1977.

The *Answer* was born during that same snowless year that saw the Vogler clan migrate to the Whistler valley. Charlie's migration had occurred four years earlier, and is notable as one of the classic "How I Came to Whistler" stories. I sat down with Charlie at Citta' in the Village Square, a bar and bistro that over the years we've come to call "the office." "I was a skier living in Thunder Bay, Ontario," Charlie told me, "and had skied in

Europe and all kinds of places, but I'd never been to the west."
He remedied that in 1972 by heading across the continent with
a friend in an MGB sports car, their unemployment insurance
cards boldly following them through the mountain passes.
Whistler wasn't their premeditated destination, though they'd
heard about its epic snowfalls and off-piste skiing from other
Thunder Bayers who'd made the trek.

It was somewhere around Banff that Charlie came across
a magazine article with the title, "Ski Bumming is Humming
in Whistler." Among the local ski bums featured in the article
were Al Davis and Lyle Featherstonhaugh. A week later Charlie
was singling his way up through the gondola line at the foot of
Whistler Mountain. "My first ride up was with Lyle and Al and
René Pacquet, these guys I'd just read about the week before.
I recognized them, and by the time we got to the top they were
going to show me around. So we skied—this was when the
highest you could get was the T-bars—and we skied Harvey's
and Boomer Bowl and Kaleidoscope and that whole thing on
the other side of the Harmony Ridge. And that was backcountry
in those days because there was no roadway back, just a cut trail
back from Burnt Stew, and I was totally thrilled."

Charlie's auspicious luck carried on past the ski day. "When
we got to the bottom at the end of the day, totally fried, totally
exhausted, this Aussie guy on a stretcher motioned to me and
asked me if I wanted a [season's] pass. And he sold me a pass
that had already been pirated. The laminations had been torn
apart and it was probably the fifth picture that had been in there.
So I got it for twenty bucks. And at Dusty's after, I also found
a place to live, which was your house, the White House at the
Hostel. And that was it. I had a pass, and a place to live on the
first day." A couple of weeks later, Charlie took the bus down
to Vancouver to pick up the rest of his stuff, and he's called
Whistler home ever since. One of his biggest challenges that

first winter was the fact that senior gondola liftee Rob Webster lived in the neighbouring hostel cabin. Charlie would run into him almost every morning in the parking lot and have to make a strained and concerted effort to keep his obviously pirated pass from being noticed.

"It was a bizarre little town," he recalled. "Really, I had never seen anything like it. I had seen hippies before and I had seen skiers before, but this town was like six hundred people, and half of them were the old Euro people like Stefan Ples and Germaine Degenhardt, and they were wonderful people. And on the other side of the coin was the hippie ski bums, which the town was full of. And then there was the more modern skiers, the guys who had become instructors and the people who had the service background, bartenders, that kind of stuff.

"Now it's hard to imagine this place being remote, but it was remote. There wasn't much going on here, a couple of gas stations. The pay phone at the 76 station was my only real way to get a hold of my family or whatever. You had to go to Squamish to get a bottle of wine, to do your laundry or cash a cheque. No, Harry McKeever would cash cheques. He had vending machines all over the valley, and he was the unofficial bank. And it [Whistler] was totally unheard of. Even people in the ski world didn't know about it. If you met Europeans in Europe skiing or in the States, it was just totally unknown, it wasn't even on maps. Garibaldi Station was the closest that was on maps. My mom phoned me and she goes, 'Whistler isn't on the map, I can't find where you live.' I'm going, 'Oh isn't it? Look for Garibaldi Station, it's not far from there.'"

It was that very remoteness that lent itself to life in the woods in a squatters' cabin. Two years after Charlie arrived in the valley, Roger Grantham "willed" him an old cabin near Function Junction. "It was a trapper's cabin actually, it was on the Cheakamus River and it had been lived in by I think one or two generations of ski bums; it wasn't being used as a trapping house. I lived there for four years, I think. And it's hard to say if I would have stayed had I not been in that situation, if I had to live in a house in Alpine with five other ski bums, but I had this really deluxe situation. It was a snug little cabin with a wood stove." Apart from the usual chores of chopping enough wood to last the winter, getting water from the river and taking a cold hike to the outhouse, the biggest challenge for Charlie was finding a place

As long as the wood stove was well fed, the squat provided all the necessary creature comforts. PHOTO COURTESY CHARLIE DOYLE

to park his pickup truck after a big snow dump. That problem could always be remedied by a well-placed case of beer for the snowplow guy, who would knock out a bigger space by the roadway entrance.

It was likely the combination of the peaceful setting, the minimal expense and the lack of electronic stimuli that enabled Charlie to continue his creative pursuits. He had attended art school in Ontario and had brought his sketchbooks and watercolours along on the trip out west. "I was just doing it wherever I was," he said. "I sort of regarded myself as a painter, even though I wasn't selling many paintings." On one of his first days in the valley, he recalled, he sat by the kitchen window in the White House and did a series of paintings of the panoramic view stretching from Mount Currie to Whistler Mountain, with Alta Lake in the foreground. "I think I eventually sold all but

one of those pieces," he said. A guitar was another key accou-
trement for a squatter (or any vagabond Canadian for that matter), and Charlie jammed with friends and sang, eventually
accompanied by the sweet vocal harmonies of girlfriend Robin
Blechman, another transplanted Ontarian who found her way
into a squatter's cabin along 16 Mile Creek at the other end of
the valley.

And then came the *Answer*. Like many good creative projects the *Whistler Answer* began as a purely imaginary enterprise.
But as acts of the imagination can do, the idea took on a life of
its own and snowballed into something much bigger. "It started
that one really bad winter when the mountain closed in January,"
Charlie remembered. "Nineteen seventy-six, seventy-seven, I
think. It opened for Christmas and then in January it closed for
a month—it was pre-snow-making, so if it wasn't happening, it
wasn't happening. A whole bunch of our friends were travelling
around the world. They just said, 'Ah, fuck this, we're off. Going

Charlie Doyle "inherited" this trapper's cabin on the banks of the Cheakamus
River from Roger Grantham in 1975. It has since been replaced by an
athletes' village. PHOTO COURTESY *WHISTLER ANSWER*

to Hawaii, going here, going there.' So we had a little group of people that I hung out with, and we had started to write a letter to friends that were in Hawaii, telling them what's going on in Whistler. And then we came up with the concept of, rather than writing the news to them, let's actually draw a front page and make it look like a newspaper." Paul Burrows had launched his weekly newspaper the previous April, so the friends took a fun jab at his oddly named *Whistler Question* by responding with the *Answer*. "And then we decided, well, we're doing this for one group of friends and we've got a bunch of different people that are in various places, so let's print them out. Then we can send them to a dozen people. Then we went, 'Seeing as we're doing this, why don't we see if someone'll give us some money and we'll put their ads beside it.'"

Here's where the letter-writing project made the quantum leap into a publishing venture. Robin Blechman took a mock-up of the front cover around town to see if anybody was interested in buying advertising. The mock-up must have looked pretty good, because she came back after one afternoon with about $2000 worth of ad sales. "So then we were forced to put twelve pages of something together," Charlie recalled. "When we'd started it was going to be the front page only, it wasn't going to be a multi-page thing. But then we had all this money and people expecting to see their ads."

Working out of an old trapper's cabin next to the Cheakamus River lent a certain old-world flavour to the publication. "It was done all by the light of kerosene lanterns," Charlie remembered. "The first half-dozen issues were totally handwritten by Robin." On the phone from her home in Toronto, Robin put it this way: "To me it was a labour of love because I was in love with Charlie. I went through a lot of pain writing that thing out. My shoulders cramped up and my fingers got really raw and we worked on it late into the night. I was just basically doing it because it was a creative thing to do and I was inspired by the editor." All the ads were done with pen and ink, Charlie said. "Not even Letraset at first, it was really like a monk's scribe. My kids look at the pictures I have of it and go, 'You look like a monk in the Middle Ages or something.' But it was bizarre even then. Most people lived in electrical houses, but we lived in a squatters' cabin so it was kind of strange."

The ski bum hippie artists who were intent on recreating the fifteenth-century print revolution originally included Charlie, Robin, Michael Leierer and, upon his return from Hawaii, Tim Smith. Production of the *Whistler Answer* usually involved a four-day bender rich in kerosene, ink, liquor, passion, paper, marijuana and/or hashish, chemicals, glue, tape and perseverance. Upon completion of the first issue, scraggily haired and bleary-eyed, the crew drove the layouts down to Claude Hoodspith's print shop in North Vancouver. Hoodspith published the *Squamish Citizen* and was interested in establishing a paper in Whistler, where he owned a cabin on Alta Lake. "So as soon as he saw that we had all these advertisers," Charlie recalled, "the first thing he asked was, 'Are these people paying you?' We're going, 'Oh yeah, yeah.' I guess he was unsure whether he was going to get the money or not for the printing job. And then also, he was always on the scam, he was trying to figure out if he could get us working for him. Because the *Question* did exist then, but it was like a foolscap thing stapled together at the corner and done on a Gestetner in Paul Burrows' basement. We'd realized if we were going to do this we had to upgrade him on the artistic presentation side, because that was more our bent."

Paul Burrows had started the *Whistler Question* after losing Whistler's first mayoral race to Pat Carleton. While Carleton had stepped forward from the Chamber of Commerce, Burrows, a ski patroller originally from England via South Africa, had been involved in the grassroots Alta Lake Ratepayers Association.

The *Whistler Answer* emerged from late nights at Charlie's squat fuelled by kerosene, passion, sticky tape and a few other substances. PHOTO COURTESY *WHISTLER ANSWER* .

The fledgling paper he and his wife Jane stapled together every Tuesday night from their Alpine Meadows home came with a promise: "We guarantee at least 15 cents worth of news and views every week and sometimes a whole lot more. We hope no issue is too hot nor controversial to be printed—items submitted will merely be edited for good taste and length as space allows." As its name suggested, the *Question*'s mission was to explore the many issues surrounding Whistler's new experimental resort government. Three-and-a-half decades later the paper is still regarded as Whistler's newspaper of record.

The *Answer* filled an entirely different role in the valley. Its inaugural edition was unveiled at the Boot Pub on April Fool's Day, 1977. Originating as it did from the fringes of Whistler's mainstream, it was able to step back and look at the workings of the town from a broad and often humorous perspective. It was also a monthly, more of a creative journal or magazine than a newspaper. Its light, irreverent tone may also have

Charlie Doyle, Robin Blechman and Tim Smith unveil the inaugural issue along with a spectacular new sign on the side of Charlie's truck, spring 1977.
PHOTO COURTESY *WHISTLER ANSWER*

stemmed from the fact that its creators had virtually no journalistic or publishing ambitions. "I don't think at any point in the *Answer*'s history did we have the illusion that we were going to overtake *Rolling Stone*," Charlie quipped. "The *Georgia Straight* wasn't in trouble because we were doing this thing."

But within the *Answer*'s artistically laid-out pages, there was plenty of entertaining and provocative material. "Even the mainstream community chuckled over it," Charlie said. "Talk to Hugh Smythe or any of the politicians of the time, the Franz Carpays, guys like Stefan Ples. Myrtle Philip loved the *Answer*, it had more to do with what she was all about." Tim Smith recalled some of the fun they had with the very first issue. "We had the three naked canoeists on the first edition. It was just an old George Benjamin photograph he'd given us. Our title was 'Trio Missing on Alta Lake.' For months people asked us if anybody had found them yet, and of course the lake was frozen solid with the thickest ice it had seen in thirty years. But it was in black and white so it must be true, right?" Charlie's editorials explored local issues and the role a creative journal might play in the community; liftee and writer Jim "Mogul" Monahan wrote fiction and other pieces; Ed Gordon (a Snow Goose bus driver), François Lepine and others took turns chronicling local occupations in the column entitled "Da Voice of da Woikin' Class." The number of contributors continued to grow with the paper: Ian Verchere, a teenager at the time, came on board with his *Localman* comic strip, in which the main character hails from the planet Vuarnet (his father was sunglass model #4002); and Bob "Bosco" Colebrook brought his erudite wit to the team after writing them a letter saying, "Your chances of a Pulitzer Prize in journalism are indeed slim without my participation."

"Also it proved to be a free invite to schmooze everything that was happening in town," Charlie said. "In those days we were actually hosting World Cup ski events, or trying to. And I remember the first World Cup downhill that was here, we had fourteen people registered on the press pass, everything from style consultants to horoscope writers to . . . We had everybody there, and all lining up to drink the Molson's. I remember I went down the first morning to register my press pass and I was already twelfth in line, I had to argue my case. 'Look I'm the fucking publisher man, this is my gig.' They're going, 'Well, we already have twelve people, Mr. Doyle.' 'Oh, well make it thirteen.' There was Bosco, Jim Monahan, everybody was lined up and fully onto the Molson's hospitality tent. We were there from dawn to dusk," he said with a chuckle.

The *Answer* writers were covering World Cup ski racing at a time when none of the major newspapers were doing so. "Nobody was printing ski news," Charlie recalled. "There was nothing in the *Vancouver Sun* even, about World Cup. But because we were the only people printing ski news we got

The early *Answer*s were all hand-lettered by Robin Blechman. "It was really like a monk's scribe," Charlie said. PHOTO COURTESY CHARLIE DOYLE

invited to events around BC, to Panorama and Big White. And because we were the only people doing it, Steve Podborski and Dave Irwin and Dave Murray would do interviews. We would arrange phone calls with them in Europe. And it wasn't like today, it took an incredible amount of organization to put through a phone call from the *Answer* office to somewhere in Switzerland. I'd be sitting there in my underwear with a beer at four in the morning doing a scratchy phone call to Steve Podborski. And they were willing, they're going, 'Hey, these guys are cool, they know skiing, they like skiing, they write about it, we'll talk to them.' And no one else was calling, basically. So we had a good voice with the actual skiers."

The *Answer* office had moved by this time to a small cabin in Alta Vista with such modern trappings as electricity and a telephone. The new location provided much better access to events in town as well as a convenient crash pad for *Answer*

The *Answer* editorial board had an ongoing tiff with the local constabulary. This marijuana plant sprouted up oddly right beside Whistler's first RCMP headquarters. PHOTO COURTESY *WHISTLER ANSWER*

staffers on their way home from the Boot Pub or the recently built village. As home to the core staffers and with an open door policy to anyone else in town, the place was going 24/7. "It was like this theatre scene going on, live, in your living room all the time. It would be compared more to an art project, a moving art installation, than a publishing venture," Charlie joked. "I remember one time I was interviewing a girl who was a stripper—that was her working-class job. So we were taking photos and it was like middle of the day, and she's hanging around the *Answer* office semi-naked. I think it was Tom Jarvis who came by to proof his ad for Beau's Restaurant—we're into the tequila and smoking dope and doing this article—and he comes by to proof his ad, and there's me and this semi-naked fox. We decided to just treat it like it was every day, right? 'Oh, Tom this is Renée, Renée, Tom.' And Tom's eyes were out to here. He was like, 'What have these guys got going?' Yeah, it was bizarre."

On another day, Ray Thibeault suddenly appeared in the yard. "I was working at my desk, looking out the window," Charlie said. "It was one of those spring days when it's rained and the sun comes out. Ray walked into the yard and placed three oranges on the grass. Everything was freshly washed by the rain and really bright, and the contrast of the orange against the green—it was like some kind of Zen art piece. Then he just disappeared as quickly as he'd arrived."

The moving-art-installation-as-magazine was not without some tensions among its creators. "Too many artistic temperaments," Charlie said, "and kind of explosive, you know. I use Hunter S. Thompson as an example, I think you could fairly compare Bosco to him. And living in the same building, it wasn't like you're going to work from eight to five. It was around you all the time." On one occasion, those explosive temperaments resulted in a fist fight between Charlie and Bosco.

In 1979 the *Answer* moved to a cabin in Alta Vista with modern conveniences such as electricity and a telephone. Here, Charlie Doyle and Michael Leierer focus on staying awake during an interview with a *Vancouver Sun* reporter.
PHOTO COURTESY CHARLIE DOYLE

Bosco attended a Chamber of Commerce dinner as the *Whistler Answer* representative the following night sporting a tuxedo and a pair of Vuarnets to cover his newly acquired shiners.

The contrast between Bosco and Tim Smith perhaps best exemplifies the diversity of characters and viewpoints that made up the *Answer*. Bosco, a six-foot-one bear of a man with an exceptionally quick wit and a penchant for grand mayhem, once expressed it to me as only he could: "Tim and I came from a different point of view. He was a little laid-back and I was a little boisterous. He was a vegetarian and I liked eating cows when they were still moving. He liked the sound of whales and I liked putting harpoons into them."

But differences of lifestyle and viewpoint aside, the creative team at the *Answer* captured the tenor of the times in Whistler. "The essence of the *Whistler Answer* for me personally was not serious journalism," Bosco said. "It was good friendship and camaraderie and trying to identify and relate the spirit of Whistler at that time. I had fun. It was a hobby. Regularly it got me some free beer and occasionally it got me laid. And for me at the time, those weren't side benefits, they were huge, colossal."

"And politicians feared us, whereas they didn't fear Paul Burrows," Charlie added. "One time we went to the mayor and the aldermen of the day and we said, 'Look, we need your pictures on file, because if we're going to do a story and it's hot on the presses and we can't get to you.' So we got a picture of [Mayor] Pat Carleton behind his desk, and the next issue we did a crude pre-Photoshop cut-out of Linda Ronstadt sitting on his knee in the Oval Office with her hand down his crotch. We were treated a little more suspect after that."

Taking off the ski boots and heading north to Meager Creek hot springs is always good for body and soul. These young soakers demonstrate their prowess at multi-tasking, *circa* 1978. PHOTO COURTESY NIGEL PROTTER

The ribald humour and irreverence became more of a problem for the publication with the leading employer in town. "The downside was that our irreverence carried over to the Mother Corp.," Charlie recalled. "It came down eventually that Whistler Mountain, and then in our later years Whistler Blackcomb, or Intrawest, chose not to advertise with us. And they wouldn't admit it. You'd confront them with it: 'It appears as though none of your people are advertising with us.' And they'd say, 'That's not true, can't be true, no. All the management make up their own decisions on this.' I'm going, 'Yeah, whatever.' But it was more important that we spoke our mind than it was having them advertise. The goal wasn't to make Whistler Mountain happy. Because there've been kind of glad-handing rags come and go—same as we have come and gone—but more people remember us for that. And then when it finally did flail apart there was no regret, it was finally a relief."

The *Rolling Whistler Review*
Just as acts of the imagination can take on a life of their own, they can also leave behind shock waves that continue to ripple through a culture. Sometimes those waves just take a little while to resurface. When the *Answer* put out its last issue in the fall of 1981, Whistler, along with the rest of North America, was heading into a recession the likes of which wouldn't be seen again until the one taking place as I write this. After seven years of intense planning, growth and physical construction in the valley, the economy suddenly went into a tailspin. While the speculation and development boom had been a virtual licence to print money for some, the abrupt change in fortune was akin to travelling down the I-5 on cruise control and somebody suddenly pulling the emergency brake. Not only was Whistler Village only half built, its centrepiece, the Resort Centre unfinished and the Whistler Village Land Company on the brink of

bankruptcy, but many smaller builders who had over-extended themselves to build spec homes suddenly lost their shirts when interest rates soared to over 20 percent.

But not everything was doom and gloom in the winter of 1981–82. The Vancouver Canucks made it to the Stanley Cup finals against the New York Islanders and I finished high school. In fact, I finished early by moving to Vancouver to live with my friend Owen Walsh's family in Kitsilano. Tired of riding the school bus to Pemberton every day for four years, I went from a small high school attended by the kids of loggers, farmers, First Nations families and ski bums to one with the progeny of Vancouver's *crème de la crème*. The abrupt change offered great opportunities for sociological study as well as a much bigger social and party scene. That same fall my brother Peter, after a few years of working, travelling and ski bumming, began his first year at Simon Fraser University. He had inherited the use of my mom's 1965 Rambler American, which was later passed on to my sister and me—a tank of a car with a three-on-the-tree manual shift and a rattan roof. It had been purchased for two bottles of dark rum from a friend of the family after he'd run into a cow with it on the way to Mount Baker.

That fall, Peter and I did many Friday-evening road trips back to Whistler for the weekend. While the Rambler hugged the two-lane strip of pavement along Howe Sound, we threw ideas back and forth and traded stories of our exciting new lives in the city. Our talks were a jam session that explored the themes of girls, literature, chemistry, travelling, DNA, life, the universe and everything. By the time we reached Squamish it was usually dark and we'd crack a road puppy and turn to the northeast. Climbing the winding hills into the pitch black of the Coast Mountains our thoughts explored the very territory we negotiated. Stories had to be created to make sense of this place and we were eager both to live them and to tell them. During those trips it became clear to me that the creative life—come hell or high water, as would almost certainly be the case—was the one worth pursuing.

Meanwhile, in Whistler and the rest of the Western world, things were beginning to turn on a whole new axis. While we had been indelibly influenced by a merry band of forest-dwelling iconoclastic artist ski bums, the valley we knew and loved was heading in an entirely different direction. For me the early eighties involved hitch-hiking from the Husky Station in Whistler down to Mexico with my friend Pierre Friele (son of gondolier and folk artist Germaine Degenhardt), travelling in Europe, Turkey, Australia and Fiji, and going to university while still trying to make the most of my free airfare, compliments of my dad's early retirement from CP Air. The baby boomers were embarking on a whole other mission in life, one that involved babies, houses, toys, real-estate investments and, for some, getting rich. It was the eighties, after all: the dawn of Reaganomics and Thatcherism; the Mulroney years; the beginning of a two-decade bender of Milton Friedman-inspired laissez-faire free-market capitalism run amok. And Whistler, well, it could have been the poster child for the decade.

In 1983 BC premier Bill Bennett had seen the importance of keeping the resort alive and stepped in with a $20-million loan for the Whistler Land Company. While the *Vancouver Sun* called him "Whistler's Mother" and others accused him of bailing out the rich, the investment in the resort municipality eventually saw a tenfold return to the province through the landholdings they took in exchange for the loan. Whistler was back on its feet and ready to run with the wolves. The change in the valley between the late seventies and the early eighties was staggering. Torn jeans and long hair were traded in for power blazers and Beemers, granola and home-cooked beans for frogurt and sushi, Colombian gold for Peruvian flake. And not only was the new boss the same as the old boss, but now he, or she for that matter, was hungry like the wolf. The curse of my generation, humbly marked by an X, is that we tend to get swamped by the wake of the baby boomer speedboat as it roars past. The blessing is that we're left with an excellent vantage point from which to observe the mania. Schooled in an earlier version of what this place could be, now it was our turn to poke an irreverent finger at the establishment.

The first issue of the *Rolling Whistler Review: A Potpourri of Local Creativity* also emerged from a small ramshackle cabin, not quite a squat, but awfully close. Just past the train station in the Southside, off in the bush to the left of Lake Placid Drive, stood two little A-frames, throwbacks to an earlier era in Whistler. The cabins, and about half of the land mass comprising the Southside, were owned by Vancouver lawyer and land baron John Taylor (son of hockey great Cyclone Taylor). For the task of repairing the roof and installing a wood stove for heat, my brother Peter and his girlfriend Margaret Hickling, both fresh out of UBC in the fall of 1986, took over one of the cabins for the paltry sum of $200 a month.

With the comforts of reasonable rent and a well-fed Franklin stove, and with the great works of English literature still singing in their heads, the couple decided that a publication seemed just the thing to churn out of the A-frame. Expo 86 had just wrapped up, Bill Vander Zalm had been crowned leader at the Social Credit convention in Whistler's own Village Square (and later won the provincial election on a platform that promised, among other things, cheaper beer) and the resort was booming once again. What seemed lacking, however, was any sense of local culture. The first issue of the *RWR* tried to fill that void by offering something other than what it saw as the predominant activities in Whistler: "drinking, skiing or marketing those two commodities." Whistler, it contended, had become little more than a "winter wonderland [with] megabucks . . . all a brief holiday fantasy," and asked the burning question, "What happens if you don't go back to the city for your weekly dose of reality? The *Rolling Whistler Review* happens, that's what!"

Despite the serious vortex of drinking and skiing, Whistler still proved to harbour some creative souls. The first issue printed a copy of liftee Chris Ellott's variation on Hamlet's soliloquy, as scrawled on the chalkboard at the base of the Blue Chair: "To ski or not to ski,—that is the question:— / Whether 'tis nobler in the morning to suffer / The knocks and bruises of outrageous black runs, / Or to take flight before a sea of moguls . . ." Ian Verchere provided some continuity from the *Whistler Answer* with a cartoon of two doctors discussing a ligament injury in progress beneath their chairlift. Young composer Mark Bell's contribution had the ungainly title "A Large Group of Words That Serve as a Title For a Piece Based on the Shortest Sentence in the Bible." (The shortest sentence, by the way, is "Jesus wept.") There was a story involving British South Pole explorer Titus Oates and a flooded, freezing Whistler apartment; a recipe to cure drunkenness that recommended three drops of eel's blood in a bottle of wine; and an assortment of poetry, all of it enlivened by Margaret's sketches and line drawings and typed up on a new machine called a computer.

The *Rolling Whistler Review* was not only eclectic, it was also sporadic. The first issue was simply dated "December," giving no indication of the magazine's publishing schedule plans. With the appearance of spring and summer solstice issues, a quarterly trend seemed to be emerging, but as one editorial admitted, the publishing date was usually determined by when an unattended photocopier could be cornered: "The *Rolling Whistler Review* is its own animal," it proclaimed. "It rears its head when it feels like it. We're only the zoo keepers." The price was also flexible: loose change, to be thrown in the accompanying jar. In terms of a business venture, the *RWR* made the *Whistler Answer* look like the *New York Times*. Advertising revenue might have set it on a more solid footing, but with the baby boomer speedboat racing for success, there was little interest among the business community in supporting a publication that seemed at odds with the upscale tone of the times.

The *RWR*'s small circulation mostly found its way into the hands of friends, but when the journal was mentioned in the *Whistler Question*, other people started to ask where they might find a copy. This surge in interest led to the third issue being printed and distributed as an insert in the *Question*. Back in Whistler for a time after travelling and studying at SFU, I became a contributor and a member of the production team. Peter had started to do some writing for the *Question*, and we were invited to lay out the issue in their office, late at night, using the technology of the day—broadsheet pages and a wax roller. We worked our magic and the paper appeared hot off the press two days later. When it did, publisher Bob Doull probably wished he'd proofed the insert before it hit the stands.

It was clearly our best effort to date. The "Almost an Editorial" explained the fortunate turn of events that enabled the *Review* to ride the *Question* "like a tick on a race horse." The contents included a fitting essay for the times, "A Eulogy for Hippiedom," by Sarah Dobell; Brett Wood chronicled the previous winter's Sextathlon on Blackcomb Mountain; Peter wrote a travelogue about touring the Olympic Peninsula in Bugsy, his van; Richard Gagne wrote an account of climbing and skiing the west couloir of Wedge Mountain with Beat Steiner and Peter Chrzanowski; there were drawings by "Mushroom" Mark MacLaurin, poems, comics and more.

My first published work, a fable titled "Mary," appeared on page three under an odd section called "Religion and Household Appliances." I had written the story while I was living in Granada, Spain, and was, I suppose, trying to make sense of the rich blend of Catholicism and liberal post-Franco fiestas. And as religious parodies are prone to do, it stirred up a hornets' nest of controversy. The local Christian community was scandalized and wrote letters to the editor of the *Question* expressing their outrage at the story, the *Rolling Whistler Review* and the *Whistler Question* for publishing it. My brother wrote back defending the piece on the grounds of its literary merit. Then later in the summer, the *Review* received a letter from someone in California who had read the story and followed the scandal. "You clearly have a satanic cult working in your community," the letter asserted, and went on to offer the services of a reputable cult-buster to deal with the problem. All in all, issue three proved a great success, though it was also the last time the *RWR* appeared as an insert in the *Whistler Question*.

The editorial zookeepers managed to tend the *RWR*

The Rolling Whistler Review appeared in many shapes and sizes between 1986 and 1991 and never failed to provoke a response. PHOTO STEPHEN VOGLER

through a few more issues the following winter, but by the spring of 1988 the journal had been reduced to a four-page guerilla-style pamphlet. "Real Estate: It's No Joke" proclaimed the front page, riffing on Nancy Reagan's anti-drug proclamation, "Just Say No." The editorial "Speculations" pondered why a Whistler condominium in new and pristine shape should appreciate in value when clearly all it could do was depreciate in condition. It went on to speculate about what might happen to Whistler if the hole in the ozone (replace with global warming) caused weather patterns to change and nudge the average temperature upward a few degrees. "Would people still want to come to Whistler to stand in the rain and ski a couple hundred feet of vertical at the peaks? What would happen to all those nice new houses and condos that the realtors and developers have artificially inflated beyond the means of most Whistlerites?" Apart from proving oddly prescient—some fifteen years later Whistler Blackcomb built the $12-million Symphony Chair to deal with that very real possibility—such writing never failed to elicit defensive letters to the editor of the *RWR* and the *Question* from local realtors and developers. Though communications were of a strained nature, we could at least boast of sparking some dialogue between disparate elements in the community.

By the fall of 1988, change was again afoot. Peter, following on the heels of the baby boomers, was about to become a father. Around the same time, he landed a weekly column with the *Whistler Question* called the "Village Voice," in which he carried on the entertaining and in-your-face style from the *RWR* for seven more years. I went back to school at SFU, but managed to put out a guerilla-style *RWR* once a year until the fall of 1991. My favourite pieces included a parodic news story on the logging of condominiums in Whistler; a review of Charlie Doyle's forty-first birthday party on Easy Street by Dunk Lopez (a.k.a. Jim Monahan); more comics, poems and rants; and a piece by Mary Talbot about the Free Box in Telluride, Colorado, which I like to think inspired Whistler's Re-Use-It Centre many years later. All in all, the *RWR* carried on the valley tradition of irreverent humour until the miraculous second coming of the *Whistler Answer*.

The *Answer*—Round Two

In the winter of 1991–92, Bob "Bosco" Colebrook made his way back to Whistler from Vancouver where he'd been working at various publications, including editing the weekly entertainment magazine *Nite Moves* for five years. Relaunching the *Answer* was in the back of his mind as a possibility, he told me over the phone from his home in Victoria, but it wasn't the sole purpose of his return. "It was my great love of Whistler," he said, with perhaps a hint of sarcasm simmering beneath his characteristic wit.

Bosco set up shop in a somewhat broken down tarp-covered trailer in the KOA campground, operated by Ruth Buzzard and conveniently located only steps from the Boot Pub. He asked Charlie over for a beer and introduced the idea of resurrecting the *Answer*. "Initially it was just to get Charlie's okay as the acknowledged rights holder of the project, to get him interested," said Bosco. Charlie recalled that it was "after quite a few beers that he convinces me we should do it again, only this time modern, with computers."

Desktop publishing was just entering the print media world in the early nineties, and it was Nigel Protter, famed Espresso Express entrepreneur, who brought his computer and graphics knowledge to the renewed publishing venture. "He leased a computer, brought it into our office at the trailer," Bosco recalled, "dumped it down and said, 'There you go.' I looked at it and, being an old-school guy, said, 'This is stupid. What's a computer for? How's that going to work on a newspaper?' It was '92. I'd just come from papers that still did manual layout using galleys, Compugraphic typesetting. But after half an hour of looking at that computer after turning it on, that was it for me. I was just in love with it. It totally consumed me because I'd been used to having so many limitations, with galleys to proof and headliners and all. And Letraset. To have that magically be able to appear at will with so many options and variables, instantaneously, it was like a toy." Final production was initially done at Nigel's place in Pemberton, Bosco said, "and he did a really great job. He was at the forefront of graphics."

As well as updating their production technology, the pair decided to approach the second *Answer* with a renewed business model. "We needed some dough," Charlie said. "We couldn't do it like we did it before, so we approached some members of

Bob "Bosco" Colebrook mulls over his next caper for the *Whistler Answer*.
PHOTO COURTESY *WHISTLER ANSWER*

the community to be shareholders. And I made sure I went to people and I told them quite clearly, 'Don't do this if it's going to take food from your children's mouths, because I don't expect you're going to get a good return.'" Despite his unorthodox sales technique, Charlie's reverse psychology drummed up investors as fast as Robin Blechman's efforts had found advertisers in the seventies. Notable town pillars such as Harley Paul, Jan Systad, Peter Alder and Rick Clare put up $2000 each to get the publication off the ground again. Less confident in the second coming of the *Answer* was Mayor Ted Nebbeling, who made a public twenty-dollar bet with lawyer Harley Paul that the *Answer* wouldn't last out the year.

Perhaps to ward off the possibility of the mayor winning his bet, or just to reflect the changing times in Whistler, this time around they "planned to be a little straighter," as Charlie put it. That plan quickly went up in smoke, however, when the first issue hit the stands on April Fool's Day, 1992. "Our first issue did have some nudity in it, but it was innocent nudity, like a woman and her baby at the nudie dock at Lost Lake," Charlie said. That photo, along with one of a streaking male skier and a short story by my brother Peter that depicted a character smoking a joint on Whistler Mountain's Peak Chair, was enough to set off a group of Whistler women who called themselves Mothers for Morality.

The controversy started when the ad hoc morality group took it upon themselves to phone all of the *Answer* advertisers to suggest that they should pull their support from the paper. Bosco recapitulated the bizarre unfolding of events in the second issue under the headline, "Book Burners, Prudes and Chuckleheads Set Up the Big Top for Three Ring Media Circus." He wrote: "The telephoners claimed to have a group of twenty-seven angry mothers. Only two names have surfaced— the twenty-five have chosen to remain anonymous—if indeed they exist at all . . . Their efforts, of course, came to naught. A big fat zero. It seems that Whistler is more of a mature, sophisticated community than they imagined."

Displeased by the efforts of the local morality squad, Bosco called John Colebourn, an acquaintance and journalism colleague at the Vancouver *Province.* Colebourn's story graced the front page of the paper with the headline: "New Mag a Rag, Say Angry Moms." "It had four of the five ingredients necessary for a good *Province* story," Bosco later wrote. "Sex, drugs, censorship and Whistler. All it was missing was a mass murder or two." The story went out on the news wire service the night before it appeared in the *Province,* and the next day, as Charlie and Bosco prepared for the *Answer* launch party, they fielded calls from Reuters News Agency, CBC Newsworld, *Maclean's,* BCTV, CBC Vancouver and, as Bosco put it, "enough radio stations to fill three bowls of alphabet soup." Between media calls they received subscription requests from as far away as Ottawa, and calls from heavy-hitting advertising agencies asking for their rate card.

The Mothers for Morality group—which was beginning to look more like one woman with a highly developed sense of moral outrage and a speed dialer—had threatened to protest the launch party, but following the *Province* story and accompanying media storm, they (or she) stayed safely away. The excitement and buzz at the launch in the Whistler Mountain Ski Club cabin matched the volume of Route 99's raunchy home-grown rock. The *Answer* was back with a bang. The free publicity was worth its weight in controversy, and the whole episode showed that the *Answer's* brand of provocative journalism was still relevant in Whistler. The congratulatory letters to the editor in the second issue hailed not only from Whistler, but also from the distant hamlet of Sooke, BC (written in verse) and the suburbs of Surrey.

In his publisher's preamble Charlie wrote, "A tiny minority trying to impose its values on the mainstream is the worst form of censorship. In our case, the result was laughable but in other parts of the world this can be more ominous." And Bosco clearly enjoyed taking the protesters to task. "Everyone was jumping on the bandwagon," he wrote, "and for what: a penis, a pair of breasts, and a marijuana cigarette . . . Personally I must confess that I was born with a penis, as were roughly half of the people I know. I do not find it particularly disgusting. In fact, on occasion it has come in quite useful—for a variety of functions. If I were to view a portion of my anatomy as disgusting, my beer gut would get the nod, and it serves no function whatsoever."

The *Answer*, with its new eleven-by-fourteen format with colour cover and over forty pages per issue, was more eclectic than ever. "The Voice of the Workin' Class" column continued to chronicle the many facets of earning a living in Whistler; Ian Verchere's *Localman* and Gord "Roxy" Harder's *Peak Brothers* comics graced the back pages; "Dog of the Month" featured the best of Whistler's canine population; local humans such as T-shirt Al Davis (his fiftieth birthday was celebrated in the early *Answer* and now it was his sixty-fifth) and Florence Petersen, founder of the Whistler Museum, were profiled; and Jim "Mogul" Monahan and Chris Kent thoroughly covered local sports, along with Peter Chrzanowski, who explored the extreme mountain variety. Rounding out the paper were "Dr. Jake," a column on (legal) drugs and health issues written by Charlie's good friend and house co-owner, Jake Onrot; a food column by chef Ross Smith; live music reviews and interviews; and correspondents Rocco Bonito and Ace Mackay-Smith, who filed stories from as far afield as Seville, Spain, Los Angeles and Jamaica.

Having survived a visit to Bosco's trailer and a night of debauchery at the Boot Pub with the editor-in-chief, Peter and I were also invited to submit material to the publication. My first piece looked at the young neo-hippies arriving in town with their tie-dyed T-shirts, hacky sacks and Grateful Dead tunes, while musing about what had happened to their hippie forefathers. After proudly cashing my first writer's cheque, I went on to become a regular contributor. I wrote about everything from travelling to biking to bands playing at the Boot, contributed short stories and parodies, and eventually debated topics with Bosco such as forestry and arts funding on the back page in a section called "Duelling Laptops."

But it wasn't until I'd spent an extended afternoon on the Citta' patio with Bosco—ostensibly to do a photo shoot for a piece I'd written about biking—that I felt I'd truly become part of the *Answer*'s dysfunctional family. More than a few drinks in, we rounded up a tandem bike and a couple of girls to sit on the back so I could whiz through Village Square, wobble-wheeling around tourists and bylaw officers, to get the shot. The hard work done, we returned to the patio for more après. By the time the sun set five or six hours later and I'd consumed far more than my first contributor's cheque could pay for, Bosco magnanimously picked up the tab on the *Answer* expense account. I'd clearly entered the big leagues of journalism, and at the same time learned a key lesson of the business: the perks often far outweigh the paycheques.

Photographer and *Whistler Answer* contributor Elwyn Rowlands in one of his rare stationary moments.
PHOTO JUNE PALEY

The *Answer* family stretched far and wide, but one of its most notorious members was photographer Elwyn Rowlands (a.k.a. Wingnut). Elwyn approached life with a shit-eating grin and an appetite for misadventure that remains unparalleled in the Whistler Valley, the Sea-to-Sky corridor and perhaps the province. He was also an excellent photographer. "He's a book unto himself," his good friend Bosco said. "He knew so many people. Others have stories that I don't even know about. But the stuff I witnessed, whew . . . At his twenty-first birthday party he got seventy-five cases of beer and he put them in his living room and he stacked them up into a big chair. He had a party, and of course everybody came over to drink the beer. He sat up at the top in the chair, and he's like pulling beers out of the armrest, he's going to drink his way to the floor, right."

Elwyn had a passion for skiing. In fact, all of his adventures tended to take place in areas of high velocity: on the mountain, in the air and on the highway. "He had a motorcycle accident," Bosco continued, "and he was in a body cast from his crotch all the way up to his neck. One of his arms is out in front in the cast, right, on a metal cast pole. And his second day back from the hospital, he goes up skiing. And he said it was great because his arm was out front like that, he could just put a beer in it . . . I mean, on and on."

When the venerable institution of the Southside Deli opened in Creekside in the late eighties, Elwyn flew his small plane low over top the deli and threw out bags of forks, knives and spoons that rained down on the opening celebrations like over-sized plastic confetti. In another of his airplane capers he crashed onto the dirt runway of the old Pemberton airfield. Following the crash, his small plane was impounded. Undaunted by the security measures, Elwyn returned with some tools, dismantled the wings and fuselage, chucked everything over the fence and drove off with the plane in his pickup truck.

But for such a fast moving character, Elwyn had a steady hand and a good eye with a camera. Not surprisingly, he had a unique guerilla style of covering events. "He would just leave on a moment's notice and go to the Olympics in Nagano." Charlie recalled, "People were going, 'Elwyn you can't just go there. There's no hotel spaces, you can't get in,' and he would just go and make it work. His whole music-photography thing, his band photos, were unparalleled, and he did that without press credentials too. Because his theory was that when you get press credentials, usually you're only allowed to shoot for a certain amount of time at the beginning of the show and then you have to stop shooting. He felt that he wasn't getting the musicians in full sweat, so he would just have a little camera and would shoot the whole night without permission."

In the pages of the *Answer*, Elwyn captured touring acts that played the Boot Pub, Buffalo Bills or the Longhorn, from Sook-Yin Lee of Bob's Your Uncle, to Ian Tyson, Long John Baldry and many more. Some of his band shots of Bob Marley and the Rolling Stones still hang in Charlie's sign-making shop on Easy Street. "Bosco hosted an exhibition of his stuff in Gastown when Bosco was working for *Nite Moves*," Charlie recalled. "It was good, it was well received." Tragically, Elwyn and his wife Kim were killed in a car accident on a particularly nasty section of Highway 99 in 2002, leaving behind their three children to the care of their relatives.

While the stable of contributors at the *Answer* was now larger and more colourful than ever before, the dynamic behind the scenes had changed considerably. The jam sessions and late-night camaraderie Bosco remembered from the first go-round—the way the paper seemed to spring organically (and chemically) from a four-day bender at the squat and appear magically at the Boot Pub after a ritual road trip to Vancouver—was no longer the modus operandi. "Everyone had grown older and taken on various responsibilities, in many cases family," Bosco said.

"By that time I did have kids," said Charlie, "and the perks of free booze and covering events and doing that whole thing— I can't say they didn't hold the allure, but it wasn't quite as possible for me to enjoy those fruits as much as I had in the earlier incarnation. I had since built and owned a house and had a family to raise and feed."

Subsequently, Bosco was not only the editor, but the trailer park captain at the helm of the *Answer*'s new ship of fools. He not only dealt with the contributors, but wrote a column, plenty of articles and the always witty captions, leaving

Mayor Ted Nebbeling (right) hands local lawyer and *Answer* investor Harley Paul a framed twenty-dollar bill and signed document to make good on his failed bet that the second coming of the *Answer* wouldn't last out its first year.
PHOTO DAVE BUZZARD

his stamp of humour on the whole publication. "I think Bosco came into his own," Charlie recalled. "I think probably from his writing perspective it was his peak, and he was a really funny writer, a really good writer." At that point Charlie still wrote the opening editorial, tackling community and local political topics such as the disturbing new trend of marketing Whistler as some kind of Disneyland in the mountains; the bizarre proposal to give golf courses a municipal tax break to the tune of hundreds of thousands of dollars; and the misguided idea of paving the trail around Lost Lake and ridding Whistler of some of its natural charms that attracted people to the mountains in the first place.

The second coming of the *Answer* survived through to its first anniversary in April 1993, when it proudly published a photo of Ted Nebbeling making good on his bet by handing a framed twenty-dollar bill and signed legal document to Harley Paul. But already there were signs that the ship was entering troubled waters. The paper had shrunk to an eight-and-a-half-by-eleven format and a slimmed-down thirty-two pages. Charlie Doyle was now listed as the founder rather than the publisher on the paper's masthead. In his editorial, he entertained the question of why he'd decided to jump back into the publishing game. "It certainly isn't the money! Ever since we spent all the investor's money, somewhere around the second issue, I've been on volunteer status." But despite his demotion after a year of "bathing in the same limelight as such luminaries as Conrad Black, Jeanneke Van Hattem and Larry Flint," Charlie summed up the worthiness of the project: "But if the world ends tomorrow, I'll go knowing it was worthwhile. We didn't tow the standard Whistler marketing schtick, didn't make too many friends in high places and probably won't win any magazine awards. What we did do and will continue to do is give local writers, artists, photographers and advertisers a place to be and in turn give discriminating locals and the occasional unsuspecting tourist a glimpse into what makes this funny little town tick."

The *Answer* foundered through the summer of 1993, and in the fall cracks started to show in the hull. Charlie's involvement steadily declined, and while Bosco had moved central headquarters from the trailer at the KOA to an apartment in Adventures West on the shore of Alta Lake, the issues continued to shrink in size. "Yeah, the next step I think was to use invisible ink; it's cheaper," Bosco deadpanned. "The problem that the second *Answer* faced is the fact that the people involved were just too good at skiing and mountain biking, and not good enough at applying themselves to trying to do any work on the paper."

Grant Lamont, organizer of the Cheakamus Challenge mountain bike race, and current town councillor, was head of advertising sales. "I know when I packed it in," Bosco said. "I was going to the post office one day and I ran into Grant and I said, 'I haven't seen you in a couple of days. What are you up to?' And he said, 'I'm just on my way over to Sechelt,' or something, 'for mountain biking for four days.' And I'm going, 'This is mid-week, what about selling ads?' And he said, 'Oh, it's all under control,' And I said, 'Well, don't bother, this isn't working . . .' You know, it's like holding on, this thing was on life support. Let's just pull the plug and make it as least painful and agonizing as possible."

Perhaps in the end, the *Answer* was not only like a performance art installation, as Charlie had described it, but like a band. It needed the various characters, the right chemistry, to hold it in a kind of working balance. It was never cut out to be a solo act. For Bosco the whole thing had been something of a strange experiment, a chance to play in his own journalism sandbox. "Don't forget, a place like Whistler, going back a few years—maybe less so today, but certainly back then—was a much more liberal and highly educated community than some. Certainly affluent. You had a lot of people who had education, and people who came through there as weekenders and tourists. [They] were basically more educated than your average resident of Surrey, and more liberal in their way of thinking, so you could pull stuff that would get you run right out of anywhere else."

In October 1993, a year-and-a-half after it had exploded back on the scene, the *Answer* published its last issue. Bosco stayed around that winter and published the *Whistler Handbook* with Kevin and Jennifer Raffler, a slim volume of history and "everything you need to know about Whistler" that predated the current *Whistler Survival Guide* that appears every year. Bosco then left town, in what some might refer to as a blaze of glory, and went on to work at publications in Rossland, the Fraser Valley, Grand Prairie (where he was reunited with his newly discovered Métis birth family), Kincolith, Prince Rupert and Victoria, not to mention half of the towns in between. "I had a really bad percentage of going to publications that went under," Bosco said with a laugh. "I don't know if there's any responsibility on my part for that happening, but it did seem to be an alarming trend."

A little over a year after the *Answer* stopped publishing, *Pique Newsmagazine* was launched by Kathy and Bob Barnett, Dave Rigler and Kevin Damaskie, all former employees of the *Whistler Question*. Its look was surprisingly similar to that of the second round of the *Answer*. "I haven't seen the *Pique* in years," Bosco said, "but from my experience, my exposure to it, I personally think it's great and I think that they had some people involved in that with real publishing experience, which has got to help." Charlie commented, "I think the tradition is being carried on by the *Pique* although in a more maudlin way, they *are* concerned about getting Intrawest's advertising whereas we didn't give a shit, which led to our demise."

The *Answer* had provided a healthy counterbalance to the publications that tended to present a rather shellacked picture of Whistler. It offered a raised middle finger to those who would Disney-fy a mountain town so long as the profit margin warranted. Calling it the way you see it might get you run out of plenty of places, Whistler included, but that strength of conviction has a way of creating ongoing reverberations. The *Whistler Answer* fostered local culture and artistic expression in Whistler in a real and lasting way. Many of its contributors went on to careers in writing, photography and the arts. And that spirit of no-holds-barred expression continues to crop up in the valley, most recently with arts collectives such as Blind Mute Productions and others down in Function Junction. Perhaps one day it will erupt again in a publication, maybe even the third coming of the *Answer*.

7

WORKING FOR A LIVING

aking music and writing stories might put a few dollars
in your pocket, entertain some unsuspecting guests
and maybe even contribute to the local culture, but
truth be told, there are more solid ways of earning a living in
a resort town. Some of the occupations most likely to put skis
on your family's feet, food in their mouths and a roof over their
heads revolve around skiing, eating and drinking, and building
or selling houses. If you've survived in the valley for any number of years, you've probably worked in one or all of these areas;
if you've stayed with it for a decade or more, chances are you've
developed one of those jobs into a profession.

My work in the restaurant industry took me from the dish
pit at L'Après all the way to fine dining at the Rimrock Café,
though only at the level of busboy; I never worked my way up
to the loftier and more lucrative position of waiter. My busing
career began in the Roundhouse in 1982, the year Whistler
Mountain took over operations from the Greeks. Slogging over

messy tables all winter (albeit only two days a week) paid off in the spring, when I was given a special mission. Me and one other busser were each put in charge of a ski patrol toboggan loaded up with soft drink canisters, sandwiches, coffee, chocolate bars and whatnot, and sent out onto the runs to extend the reach of Whistler's food services. That was the basic idea, but the soft drink setup made the toboggans too heavy to manoeuvre very far on skis. Instead, on sunny days I'd drag my sled as far as the light board near the top of the old Red Chair and stab my sun umbrella into the snow. The sales were brisk at "Steve's Good Eats," as my sign proudly read, and I got to see almost everybody on the mountain. The tip jar also filled up quickly. Depending on my mood and aspirations on that particular day, the label on it either read "Help Send Steve to Europe" or "Help Send Steve to University."

I completed my ski instructor's course at the end of that winter and spent the next two seasons teaching skiing. But to augment my income in the spring of 1985, I returned to the restaurant business. Bob Dawson was a ski instructor who had recently opened the Creekhouse Restaurant with chef Rolf Gunther in the Creekside Lodge across the highway from the old Gulf gas station. Bob hired me on as a busboy. The Creekhouse served good hearty fare such as pasta and burgers, and attracted a loyal clientele of locals and visitors. The serving staff plied the large downstairs room and the smaller loft above like a well-oiled machine. They were friendly and professional, but still real—no Keg waiter spiel here. The kitchen, where Hatto Horn, John Lee, Brenda Neilsen and others worked with Rolf, was equally talented, and together the staff at the Creekhouse created a team approach to good restaurateuring that carries on to this day.

In 1986 Rolf and Bob left behind the Creekhouse and opened the Rimrock Café & Oyster Bar just across the highway in the Highland Lodge. The Highland, which opened with twenty rooms, a restaurant and a bar in 1965, was one of Whistler's first lodges. The upstairs barroom, now part of the restaurant, has the feel of a quaint New England inn that's not afraid to let its hair down and party when the mood strikes. The big stone fireplace has listened in on many a tall tale and the rafters have felt the grip of countless committed ski bums vying to win a bottle of tequila in the Highland's legendary Rafter Hanging contests. My first experiences at the Highland Lodge involved watching movies from the rocks outside the window with my friend Mark MacLaurin—you had to be a resourceful fourteen-year-old to find entertainment in the valley in those days. Peter the Swede ran the bar and restaurant at the Highland and started hosting Sunday jazz nights that were then carried on by the Rimrock Café. Local musicians Karen Graves, Lonnie Powell, Mark Schnaidt, Tom McCoy, Marc Bombois, Donald Crook, Steve "Speedo" Marion, Trisha King and Helen Thibault comprised the regular house band, supplemented occasionally by Doc Fingers and other feature acts from Vancouver. The joint was always jumpin' in a cool, finger-snapping kind of way, and anyone with jazz aspirations could join in. Karen Graves later moved to Vancouver to play saxophone, clarinet and sing with Vancouver's best jazz musicians. When they weren't busy on the main stage, some visiting jazz greats played the Highland Lodge during Whistler's first, best and only real summer jazz festival in the eighties. But back to the Rimrock.

Bob and Rolf brought their entire team with them from the Creekhouse and traded the burgers and Caesar salads for more upscale items such as ahi tuna, shucked oysters, lobster bisque and filet mignon. By the time I began busing there in 1988, the team had begun to grow into a family of restaurateuring ski bums. Most of them are still there today, having worked, skied, partied and windsurfed together for a quarter of a century. If there's a Ph.D. student out there who's looking for a thesis topic along the lines of "Restaurant to Real Mountain Riding: The Integration of Work and Play in a Coast Mountain Ski Resort," here is all the material they'll need.

Pat "Puzz" Rowntree

Pat Rowntree's story captures perfectly the life of a ski bum–professional server. I first met Puzz in the early eighties shortly after she arrived in the valley. We recently sat down for a drink at Brandy's in the village to examine the last quarter century of her life, beginning with her classic "How I Came to Whistler" story. With a bachelor's degree in Environmental Studies from the University of Waterloo, the tall, young, raven-haired lass moved to Vancouver to do an MBA at Simon Fraser University. She stayed with her sister, who also happened to rent a weekend cabin at Whistler. At the end of the first week of classes, one of Pat's profs announced that it was the last day to get tuition fee

Local waitress, ski bum and rafter-hanging queen Pat "Puzz" Rowntree backstage at the Rimrock Café. PHOTO COURTESY PAT ROWNTREE

refunds. "I walked to the registrar's office like a zombie and quit," she said.

Next thing she knew, Pat was in Whistler living full time in a weekend ski cabin where she paid only a few hundred dollars for the season. It was 1982, a great snow year. She started waitressing at L'Après at the Creekside base and skiing every day. Soon she was dating her manager, Chris "Freddie Boy" Bahry, originally from Kimberley and now her husband and cohort in ski bumming, windsurfing and travelling some twenty-five years later. "My alma mater phoned recently after a reunion to check on everybody," Pat said. "Chris told them, 'All you need to know is, she's a ski bum.' I have a degree in environmental studies and I've never worked a day in that field in my life. I loved skiing, and waitressing gave me the lifestyle. It's not something I do *until* I get a real job; it *is* my real job."

Pat's transition from serving at L'Après to the Rimrock Café involved another feisty and decisive moment in her life. "In 1984 I quit Dusty's in a rage," she told me. "It was too busy, there weren't enough staff and they ran out of beer mugs. I flung my tray at Curtis the bartender and walked out. I started driving home and I picked up Bob Dawson hitchhiking by the old Gulf station. He offered me a job at the Creekhouse and I've been working for him and Rolf ever since."

When the two restaurateurs left the Creekhouse and opened the Rimrock, Pat moved with them, along with coworkers Leslie Burgess, Deanna White, Kenny White, Sue Clark, Hatto and Roberta Horn, John Lee, Don Butler and others, most of whom still work there today. "Rolf is European," Pat said. "People in Europe treat restaurant work as a profession. It's starting to happen here. There are a lot of old waiters in this town—I'm not the oldest," she joked. "We have fun at the Rimrock. We have staff ski days. Some of us do road trips to the Gorge in Oregon."

And the waitressing gig meshes well with her urge to travel, Puzz said. "You can get chunks of time off. We go to Hawaii for windsurfing." One winter she and Chris, who is also a bartender and server, travelled to Nepal and India, then on to the west coast of Australia for three months of wine touring and windsurfing. "We went to Chamonix for the month of April in 2000—got about six powder days out of it—then carried on to Spain, Portugal and Morocco to windsurf." Working in the restaurant profession also enabled them to buy a house in the valley, back in 1985, for $74,000.

Pat's training program of skiing, windsurfing and waitressing has not only kept her in good shape, it's also developed a strong pair of wrists that have served her well in many areas of life. It should be noted that Puzz was once the proud winner of that bottle of tequila in the Highland Lodge Rafter Hanging contest.

Banjo Picks and Mushroom Caps

Among the cast of characters in the Whistler bar and restaurant industry, there are few practitioners with more character than my old friend Mushroom Mark. Some time after our caper-filled teen years, Mark moved into various squatters' cabins in an era when squatting was no longer condoned or even looked upon with a blind or forgiving eye. Eventually he started working at various restaurants in the valley, but unlike Puzz and others with an allegiance to a particular establishment, Mark operated more as a freelancer. He roamed among different restaurants and bars, developing his skills as a server, cook, bartender, snow sculptor and, more recently, sommelier. I hadn't realized the extent of Mark's talent until he showed up at my fortieth birthday party with a bottle of champagne, which he sabred open with the foot of a wine glass. By the time the sun rose there was also a full-sized bar sculpted out of snow in the backyard.

In his apprentice years of snow sculpting, Mark would often spend long evenings in the village or elsewhere in the valley, creating mythic creatures—and sometimes entire villages—that would greet the tripped-out clubbers who spilled into the village at two or three in the morning. Snow sculpting may seem a tangential skill in the restaurant world, but it has served Mark well over the years. Special events on the mountains put on by wineries, breweries or distilleries often include snow sculptures as part of their display setup. Mark has also sculpted characters for the kids at Merlin's Castle on Blackcomb and in the Magic Forest on Whistler. Following in the footsteps of his mother, Isobel MacLaurin, who painted the Roundhouse murals in exchange for season's passes, Mark has traded his snow sculpting skills for many seasons' worth of skiing.

Apart from his other abilities, Mark has always been part of the local music scene. Our first jam sessions go back to when we were about fourteen and Mark would come over from his parents' cabin at Alpha Lake to jam in the little shotgun shack at the Tyrol Lodge. While I only knew a few guitar chords, Mark had some musical background from playing in the stage band at his school in Port Coquitlam. Once we even took our show on the road, dragging our gear to the empty train station at Creekside to try to reproduce the full echo effect of a stadium rock concert sound. Fortunately there was nobody around to hear us. Years later, Mark would show up at the jams at Citta', the Boot and the Longhorn, sometimes armed only with his considerable booming voice, other times with a trumpet as well. When I played a lot of gigs around town, Mark was always up for taking the stage and belting out the Who's "My Generation" or Steve Miller's "Space Cowboy." Later, when I played with the Hounds of Buskerville, Mark would occasionally show up part way through the gig dressed in a snappy suit, his trumpet in tow. Our college-educated, jazz aficionado horn players with

Mushroom Mark at Merlin's patio with one of his snowy creations that earned him the season's pass hanging around his neck. PHOTO COURTESY MUSHROOM MARK

their carefully worked out horn lines would look down their noses as Mark sprayed a little WD-40 on his trumpet to get the stuck valves working. But stage presence is half the battle, and given the opportunity to blow a solo, Mark was always well received by the crowd. The Hounds were playing at the Boot Pub one night (and I'm quite sure I wasn't hallucinating) when Mark skied in through the front door. He had been at some late, on-mountain party where he'd probably built a snow bar, and he was wearing a flashy suit and carrying his trumpet. He slid up to the bar for a drink, goggles still on his head, then made his way up to the stage to blow some horn with the band. I can't remember when exactly he clicked out of his bindings, or whether the saxophone players had to watch out for sharp ski edges as well as the overspray of WD-40, but he certainly captured the attention of everyone in the bar.

Mark's moniker of "Mushroom" goes back to his earlier, wilder days of picking the many varieties of fungi that grow in the Coast Mountain region. He actually does have an extensive knowledge of all edible varieties, but after picking large quantities of a certain small-capped genus, he developed an allergy to their potency. As every obstacle is an opportunity for innovation, Mark overcame the problem with style. "So I figured out the best way to pick 'em," he told me, well into the evening at my fortieth birthday party. "You wear surgical gloves and banjo picks, it's incredible!" Indeed.

The Lumberyard

The third typical way of making a living in Whistler, or any mountain town for that matter, is by working in construction. My own early exposure to the building world was during my very first job at age fourteen at Garibaldi Building Supplies. Every Saturday throughout the fall of 1978 I showed up at the building supply yard across the tracks from Mons, where the second hole of the Nicklaus North golf course now sits. Remuneration: $2.65 per hour. I was given the tasks of sorting piles of lumber or moving them from one seemingly random location to another, which had me wondering whether the work was really necessary, or simply designed to keep me busy and build some bulk on my skinny frame. When the lumber had been moved around enough times I would work sorting the nail bins or loading kiln-dried lumber and fifty-pound boxes of nails into customers' cars and trucks. Occasionally, if I was required go into the store to help a customer find a particular item, there was a good possibility of running into the owner's daughter Susie, an older woman of sixteen or seventeen, and perhaps even exchanging a few nervous words with her.

Apart from those glorious moments, my favourite part of working at Garibaldi Building Supplies was delivering lumber with Dick Fairhurst. Dick was already close to retirement age by then, a soft-spoken, hard-working man whose kids, David and Carol, were the same age as my brother and sister. When it came to construction in Whistler, Dick was as old school as they come. In the fifties he built the Cypress Lodge (now the Whistler Hostel) and the cabins next to it on Alta Lake. He and his wife Kelly ran the guest cabins and lodge, which doubled as an unofficial community centre and party site for everyone at Alta Lake. The Fairhurst family home, the White House, was on the upper portion of the property, and is the same abode where my wife Peggy and I have been raising our children for the past fifteen years.

Dick was a keen builder who wasn't afraid to experiment with new forms of infrastructure at Alta Lake. He and Andy Petersen installed not only the first piped water system from Scotia Creek on Sproatt Mountain, but also the first hydroelectric generation setup from the same waterway. These projects required a small amount of blasting and, as Andy recalled, neither he nor Dick had any experience with explosives. After they set their charges, they simply lit the fuse and ran down the hill. Hiding under cover in the forest, they watched as chunks of granite sailed skyward, bouncing off the transmission wires high above them. It appeared that they'd slightly overestimated the quantity of dynamite they'd needed for the job.

Dick also created the first lift-serviced skiing in the valley. Directly above the Cypress Lodge property under the power lines, he installed a tow rope powered by a Ford 450 engine, which dragged three skiers at a time up its five-hundred-foot length. When Whistler Mountain opened in 1966, Dick worked as one of its first ski instructors. After one of his pay-cheques from Jim McConkey amounted to twenty dollars after two weeks of work, he decided to return to the more lucrative avails of construction.

On Saturday afternoons in 1978, the oldest and youngest member of the Garibaldi Building Supplies staff would load lumber and other supplies onto an old flatbed, then cinch it down with wide burlap straps threaded through mounted ratchets. We'd deliver to houses under construction in White Gold Estates or other newer subdivisions and touch base with the builders who were slowly filling the valley with more and more homes.

Actual work in house construction began for me the summers after I'd finished high school. I got a job wiring houses with electrician Gary Carr, whom I'd worked for in 1980 on Blackcomb Mountain. Gary is a well-travelled and very laid-back Australian who arrived in Whistler over thirty years ago. His approach to contracting was markedly different from many others in the construction trades. Gary worked to live, he didn't live to work, and this was probably why we got along so well. Once Gary got a contract to wire a house, he'd give me a call and suggest that we start on it "some time next week." That timeline would often slide back a week, which was fine with

me, as I was usually working on some writing project or practising my music. We'd start at the very respectable hour of nine
o'clock, but once the job got under way and we could see that it
was moving apace, the start time could become more flexible.
"Why don't I give you a call between nine and ten tomorrow?"
Gary would say in his mellowed Australian accent. A couple of
phone calls back and forth the following morning might result
in an eleven o'clock start or, if it got too close to noon, we might
not get to work until after lunch. And when Gary had a softball
game, we were sometimes forced to quit early. Still, we successfully wired dozens of houses in the valley and as Gary used to
say, "I still get a charge when I flip the switch and see the place
light up." Gary now lives with his wife Annie in Pemberton,
and manages the nearby Rutherford Creek Power Station.

The Al Schmuck School of Construction

Knowing how to frame a building is a skill well worth having, and I'm glad to say I learned it from one of the best, Al
Schmuck. Al was a schoolteacher in Vancouver before he
tossed in that career in exchange for a life in the mountains.
He worked winters as one of Whistler Mountain's first professional ski patrollers and in the summers he built houses,
beginning in 1971 with his own place high above Drifter Way in
Alpine Meadows. Many friends from all parts of the world have
climbed the over one hundred stairs up to Al's West Coast-style
home with the incredible view of Wedge and Armchair and all
the mountains on the east side of the valley. It has been home
not only to Al, his wife Trudel and stepdaughter Bianca, but to
many others over the years, including Gary Carr.

Al called his company Intermountain Construction, perhaps wisely leaving his surname out of it, but I've always
thought of it as the Al Schmuck School of Construction. This
notion was borne out at Al's memorial at Gary and Annie's

place in Pemberton last summer, where hundreds of friends gathered from many parts of the world to pay their respects to their good friend who was suddenly taken from them in July 2008. He was vibrant and seemingly fit as a fiddle to the end. As story after story was told, it became apparent that about half of those in attendance had learned to swing a hammer from Al. He never did leave his teaching career behind, he just took it with him into a different context. One former labourer on Al's crew commented that with all the mistakes he'd managed to commit during his first summer, including nailing a whole row of rafters into the wrong position, Al never raised his voice in protest. With Zen-like patience, he simply introduced him to the carpenter's best friend, the nail puller, with which the young man spent the next half-day undoing his mistake.

I remember working for Al on Harley Paul's house in Whistler Cay Heights in 1988. Late one Friday afternoon I was sent to Garibaldi Building Supplies with Al's ancient red Volkswagen pickup to get rough cedar fascia boards. The crew was going to work late that day to get a head start on install-ing the fascia before the roofers arrived the following week. I was supposed to pick up some drinks for the crew on the same journey. After successfully loading the sixteen-foot two-by-tens, I stopped at Nesters for the drinks. Looking at my load, I sud-denly wondered if it wasn't actually two-by-twelves that I was supposed to have picked up. A glance at my note confirmed my mistake, but when I got back to GBS the gates were closed for the weekend. Not wanting to sabotage the whole effort, I decided to get resourceful. There was just enough space to slide boards under the fence, so I unloaded the entire truck and pushed the two-by-tens back into the yard. Then I climbed the fence, careful not to get hooked on the barbed wire, brought out the two-by-twelves and loaded them onto the pickup. The whole operation probably took an extra forty-five minutes, and

Al Schmuck always maintained a good sense of humour on the work site. Here he took golfing to a whole new level while constructing this home on Blueberry Hill. PHOTO COURTESY TRUDEL GUNTHER

by the time I arrived back at the job site, the crew had already packed it in for the day. I've worked on construction sites where a mistake that costs time and money can result in two-by-fours and hammers flying across a half-constructed building. Al took things in his usual stride and chuckled at my sorry tale. In fact, he looked relieved to see me. When I hadn't returned after an hour, he thought I might have lost the pickup and the load over the bank at Nesters. The handbrake didn't work so well on the old Volkswagen.

One of my favourite stories from Al's memorial was delivered by Nigel Woods. Nigel started Coast Mountain Excavation many years ago, and now runs the Riverside Campground with his wife Buffy. In the early eighties he managed to take possession of one of the two small islands in Alpha Lake and constructed a suspension bridge to it so that he could build his family home there. These are the same islands that Mushroom Mark, his sisters Jill and Sue, my sister Vicky, cousin Sylvia and I would camp out on in the summers as teenagers to watch the Perseid meteor showers. Al was contracted to build the Woods' house and I worked on the crew for a brief time.

What Nigel recalled so clearly was the day he stopped in at the work site and Al approached him with a slightly altered plan for the kitchen. He carefully explained how pushing out one wall another metre would greatly enhance the whole design. The decision had to be made immediately. After pouring over the blueprints, Nigel looked at Al and asked him how much it would cost. That's when he realized that Al, who had a habit of wearing very little while working on hot summer days, had taken this penchant to new lengths on the isolated island; he was standing in front of Nigel with nothing on but his tool belt. Not wanting to discuss the matter any longer than necessary with this balding, naked contractor, Nigel immediately agreed that the cost sounded reasonable. Mission accomplished, Al turned around and climbed back out onto the posts and beams, leaving Nigel to ponder his decision, along with the image of Al's hairy little ass.

The building skills I learned at the Al Schmuck School of Construction have come in handy over the years. When our twin daughters Katie and Melissa were born, I added a bedroom onto the tiny cabin we were renting at the time, bringing its floor size to six hundred square feet. More recently I was in need of a small outbuilding to use for a writing space so I could get out of the house during the day, as I was experiencing some allergy problems. As I built the little, hundred-square-foot shed where I'm now finishing this book, I often thought of Al, who had recently passed away. It had been a long time since I'd framed a wall, but as I progressed, the necessary skills always came to me just as I needed them—things like remembering to let the plywood overhang the bottom of the wall so it overlaps the floor joists, or to leave expansion spaces when nailing up the sheets of plywood sheathing.

I began the project as usual by gathering discarded building materials from construction sites. On one such sojourn, local construction worker and song-and-dance man Brian Lamport set me up with a hard hat and a fluorescent vest for safe foraging in exchange for a case of beer. "Just take material from the bank there where they throw the scrap," he said, as we walked through the large condo project where the Boot Pub once stood. There were plenty of useful two-by-fours and two-by-sixes and even some full sheets of three-quarter-inch plywood. I parked a borrowed pickup truck inside the fenced-in construction site and walked around like one of the workers. In the end, it was one of those sheets of plywood that nearly led to the loss of my undercover status. I tried taking it up the steep gravel bank, but had to lift it flat above my head because the corner would jam into the bank in the traditional sideways carrying position.

With one step to go to the top, I made a lunge to beat the slippery gravel. The gravel won. My feet slipped out and back, the plywood went up and then, as one might expect, it came down onto my head. It was fortunate I had the hard hat on, because it cracked loudly as I was knocked flat onto the gravel slope and slid most of the way back down it as my shirt and vest slid up. Feeling the burn of gravel streaks down my belly and forearms, I lay pinned under the plywood until I was ready, and able, to emerge. Al Schmuck would have enjoyed a good chuckle over that one.

Nancy Wilhelm-Morden

While many a professional career was left behind in one city or another for the allure of living in the mountains, some Whistlerites managed to bring their professions with them. A few even managed to gain the necessary occupational credentials while living in a town full of impassioned ski bums. Nancy Wilhelm-Morden went from pumping gas at the 76 station and living in a squatter's cabin to becoming a lawyer, a multi-term Whistler councillor and a cracking good political columnist for the *Whistler Question*.

Fresh out of high school in Kitchener, Ontario, Nancy first came to Whistler for a two-week holiday in the summer of 1973. Ted Morden, her future husband and sweetheart since the age of fourteen, had come out a few weeks earlier to get a job logging at the Malloch and Moseley camp at Function Junction, where they lived in one of the logging camp bunkhouses. Ted planned to stick around to work and then ski for the winter while Nancy would return home for her first year at the University of Waterloo.

"I called home on the last day before my flight," Nancy said, fresh-faced from a morning of skiing as we sat by the wood stove in their Alpine Meadows home. "My parents were horrified. Ted and I found a little basement suite in Creekside. We got a dog, of course." The couple spent the winter and the following summer there before Ted headed off to Europe and Nancy went home to complete her first year at Waterloo. By the spring of 1975 they were back and looking for a place to live in a town with virtually no accommodation. "There were these people living in the bush," Nancy said, "so Ted decided to build a squatter's cabin. He built it from scratch, and didn't know anything about building except what he'd learned working on the Tamarisk or 'Take-a-risk' condominiums."

Their cabin was tucked in the forest next to Crabapple Creek, a kilometre south of the garbage dump, a spot that would later be developed into the Brio neighbourhood. "We lived there until we moved here in 1979. Those four years allowed us to save money to build this house and to go to university." Nancy went to Simon Fraser three days a week and waitressed, skied and studied by kerosene lamp in the squatter's cabin the other four. "The squatting experience was amazing," she said. "It was sheer dumb luck. There was nothing here at the time but this massive mountain, and it was so beautiful and clean. And the place started growing up—if I can put it that way—just as we were."

Ted and Nancy's house backs onto a forest, with a small creek running by. Looking out the window at the snow falling on the idyllic setting, I get the sense that they didn't so much trade in the old Whistler lifestyle as incorporate it into their current one. I ask Nancy how she went from squatting, skiing and waitressing to setting up a law practice in town. "I had wanted to be a lawyer all my life," she said. "If Whistler hadn't grown up too I wouldn't have been able to set up here. When I look back it was quite fortuitous." Nancy was accepted into law school at UBC as Whistler was suffering through its early eighties recession. After she was called to the bar in 1984 she began practising law in Vancouver four days a week. By 1986 daughter Sarah was born, Nancy was a member of Whistler town council and she was still working in Vancouver. It was all way too much to handle, and she made the decision to set up a law practice in Whistler.

"I'm a litigator, I like trial work, and I thought I might be kissing all that goodbye for a country practice with lots of solicitor's work. But it was anything but that," she said. One of many fascinating trials Nancy worked on in the valley involved the status of the old Mons Road, for which she interviewed some pioneers from the Green Lake area. "One of these guys recalled

Nancy Wilhelm-Morden and Ted Morden outside their idyllic squat next to Crabapple Creek in what is now the Brio neighbourhood. PHOTO COURTESY NANCY WILHELM-MORDEN

the old mink farm where Nicklaus North is now, and another told stories of the old Mons post office—that when there was only one letter it would be taped to a potato and thrown from the passing train."

In the world of a one-time squatter ski bum, four-term Whistler councillor and litigator with local and international clients, there is no shortage of good stories. While it has no legal implications, one of Nancy's favourites involved a restless three-legged dog: "It belonged to a guy named Peter Helicopter, who would go skiing at Creekside and leave the dog at the base. Bored of waiting at the old L'Après, the three-legged dog would religiously hobble back to the highway and hitchhike home to Function Junction." And that, Your Honour, is a true Whistler story.

Derek Rhodes

Just across the tracks from where the potato letters used to fly off the train lies a small industrial site known as Mons. Barney's Automotive and Sabre Rentals occupies the bottom of the largest metal building, and up on the second floor nestled under the roof sits a small ski-tuning shop. This is where Derek Rhodes works his overnight magic of keeping Whistlerites' skis and boards gliding smooth and true. The big steel roof beam that divides the room is spray bombed with the shop's name, Profile, in the same graffiti-art style as on the freight cars that whip past the building.

As we talk, Derek cuts out a nasty gouge from the base of a ski and welds a piece of black plastic into place until the damage is invisible. People stop in to drop off skis and exchange stories about their day on the mountain. The shop has a festive atmosphere, and with work starting at 4:30 in the afternoon, Derek still has time to get in plenty of skiing and boarding himself.

"The way I see it, every ski town needs a little back-room ski-tuning guy where you can get a good deal and sit down and have a chat over a beer." The mountain shops focus on rentals, he said, and they have a lot of first-year employees. "I do a better job. People come here and they know it's me. I grind every single ski that comes through here."

His story of arriving in Whistler is a typical one. Straight out of high school in 1990, he and two buddies drove out west to visit a friend in Vancouver. They started applying for jobs at ski areas in the fall—Lake Louise, Panorama and finally Whistler. Derek was hired on the spot at Jim McConkey's Ski Shop, and started earning twice the wage he'd earned at a bike shop in Halifax that summer.

After ten seasons at the mountain, Whistler's ski and party scene was starting to wear a little thin. Derek worked for a year at the front desk of Barney's Automotive and a few months at the High North Summer Ski Camp, then shipped his stuff back to Nova Scotia with the idea of working a winter in France. But as he waited for an EU passport in Halifax, he began noticing photos of all his friends from the summer camp in the ski magazines. "I got homesick for Whistler," he said. "I'd partied with them all summer." When his EU passport didn't come through, the gravitational pull of Whistler was too much and Derek headed back west. Taking the

Derek Rhodes works his magic on a pair of boards at his upstairs ski tuning shop in Mons. PHOTO TOSHI KAWANO

long way round, he did a 20,000-kilometre road trip through the southern United States before returning to his favourite Coast Mountain town.

"I'd just turned thirty so I was starting to get antsy about what to do," he said of his early mid-life crisis. Whatever he would end up doing he knew he didn't want to go back to working at the mountain. "For some reason I remembered this empty loft space above Barney's with a bunch of garbage bags in it. And I knew it had three-phase power for industrial use." Derek drew up a business plan, borrowed $10,000 on a line of credit and opened in December 2003 with a stone grinder, side edger, bevelling unit and two workbenches. And the rest, as they say, is ski-grinding history.

Just to kept things interesting, Derek has spun his interest in surfing into a sideline. He buys foam blanks and shapes the boards, selling a few and making them for friends. "It keeps me connected to the surf world when I can't go," he said, pointing to an old autographed Barnfield board that hangs in the rafters of the shop.

On living in Whistler for nearly twenty years, Derek said, "Those first five years you're just givin' 'er, skiing or boarding and partying. But then you start to see there's other people with things on the go. I did my search to go elsewhere and it didn't work out. So I had to decide, how am I gonna do it? I feel like I'm on the second tier now. Like I'm part of the community and I have a place in it. I even voted last time."

Ace Mackay-Smith

Ace Mackay-Smith is living proof that there are a thousand different creative ways to make a living in a mountain town. The first thing I noticed on entering her Twin Lakes condo was that there wasn't a single flat space on which to place my notepad, let alone the beer she'd offered me. "Welcome to the pirate ship," she said with a twinkle in her eye and that schoolgirl charm that keeps her looking eternally eighteen. The portside wall is covered with old ski photos of her mom and dad; her father was a ski instructor and eventual manager and part owner of Tod Mountain near Kamloops. Ace pulls out her ski boot from when she was two years old—a nice, French-made, two-buckle affair that would look handsome hanging from a rearview mirror. Just forward of the kitchen, her sewing machine is surrounded by fabric and the dance costumes she makes. Hats adorn the stairwell wall, and an original George Littlechild painting hangs on the starboard forewall. "Uncle George," she said, used to do pastel sketches of Ace and her brother when they'd play with him at her grandmother's (and George's foster parents') house in Edmonton. Considering that Ace's pedigree is rich not only in ski lore but also in creative arts, it's really no wonder that she became Whistler's first and foremost go-go dancer.

Apart from junior ski racing and a few family holidays, the Whistler life started for Ace in 1987. She'd travelled for nearly a year in Europe after high school and came back to work at Expo 86 in Vancouver. One of the managers of the Irish pub where she waited tables was opening a pub in Whistler and offered her a job. Having worked in the French Alps at Courchevel the previous winter, she already had it in her head to live in a ski resort. After that first waitressing job she moved to Citta' and within a year was go-go dancing at Tommy Africa's.

"I remember there weren't many girls in town," she said. "I'd look around in a bar and see three other girls. That's maybe why they wanted to do it." I pointed out that most of Whistler's male population was smitten by her fluid moves and disarming smile. "They were drunk," she quipped modestly. "I was one of them," her boyfriend, Wicked Lester, piped up from near the helm of the ship where he was burning me a music CD.

"Being a girl in a bar is always kind of like that anyway,"

Ace "Longstocking" Mackay-Smith replete with waterwings at her self-produced "Good ol' Fashioned Rave" in April 2007. PHOTO TOSHI KAWANO

Ace said. "When I dance I think more of the women, looking at them and smiling at them. If they're having fun, then the guys are having fun." A night of dancing at Tommy's or elsewhere usually involves three forty-minute sets, Ace said. "It seems like a stupid job, but I get paid to work out. I don't really do anything else to stay in shape—just skiing and dancing."

Those two activities have led to plenty of other creative pursuits in Ace's life. When the female skier in Greg Stump's *License to Thrill* ski movie was injured, Ace happened to be working at Christine's on Blackcomb and was asked to fill in. That role led to years of skiing, shooting and doing still photography in the film business and to a creative and sometimes jet-setting partnership with Greg Stump that carried on for a decade. More recently, her five-minute animated short featuring a Real Girl doll (batteries not included) who schools her admiring weekend warrior in the ways of mountain life won the seventy-two-hour Film Makers' Showdown in 2002.

Ace formed AMProductions with partner Michael Ziff and began throwing the closing parties for the nascent World Ski and Snowboard Festival. "Raves were really creative back then," she said with a hint of nostalgia. "We'd do themed DJ parties— PlayHouse, Hullabaloo, Deep, Heaven—integrating things like live painters, drummers, visuals, fashion shows, sandboxes, giant teddy bears, light tunnels, bubble wrap on the floor, whatever we could think of that would make people go, 'Wow!'"

Some of those parties were held at the Alpen Rock and the Conference Centre and are permanently etched on many a local's and visitor's mind. One year she produced the Big Air show at the base of Whistler with dancers hanging on silk strings à la Cirque du Soleil, African drummers, DJ Vinyl Ritchie (a.k.a. Wicked Lester) and vocalists, an eight-year-old blues guitarist and a troupe of tiny karate kids from Function Junction.

Then there's her most recent incarnation as DJ Foxy Moron. "I had my own records and my mom's and dad's old records," Ace said. "I was into music. dancing all those years and listening to DJs. I learned through osmosis."

So where is Ace's pirate ship headed next? It's hard to say, but with this go-go dancing, Pippi Longstocking of a ski bum at the helm, it's bound to keep plying Whistler's creative waters for many years to come. And who knows, working as a creative artist in Whistler might one day become as common as waiting tables or banging nails.

8

THE SKI BOOT

Many of my early experiences in Whistler involved looking in through a window or a door on a world I wasn't
yet old enough to take part in. In this regard, my first
Boot Pub experience followed the same pattern as watching
movies through the window at the Highland Lodge, or listening to Doug and the Slugs outside The Keg. Just inside the back
door of the old Ski Boot Motel, later known as the Shoestring
Lodge, was another door that led directly into the pub. It was
there that I caught my first impressions of the mysterious
world inside: a band setting up on stage; a few patrons standing
by the bar; some old ski boots perched on the high shelves; and
the aroma of the beer-stained shag carpet and red terry-cloth
table mats.

I've quite likely augmented those early memories with my
many other visits over the years, partly because the first time I
looked in the door of the Boot Pub was also the first time I got
drunk. It was a May 24 long weekend, the time when winter

was properly ushered out of the valley and spring was rung in with pagan enthusiasm and abandon. Under the influence of that annual spring thaw ritual, my friends Matt Bolton, Brook Calder and I found a bootlegger to score us a case of Molson Canadian off-sale from the pub. We sat on the rock just behind the back door and proceeded to discover the effects of 5 percent lager on the teenage brain. As I recall, I never made it to the fourth stubby (my share), and the aftermath involved perambulating around the valley, climbing water towers, wading though creeks and exploring the roof of The Keg at the Mountain— generally going as low and as high as was humanly possible and, thanks perhaps to some lucky stars, remaining alive and in one piece. After sleeping over at Matt's house (which later became the *Whistler Answer* office), I was treated to an afternoon at the Christianna Inn, replete with wet T-shirt and belly-flop contests, a live band on the patio and a couple of hundred revellers on the roof. But back to the Boot.

A good pub is like a home away from home. The Boot, surrounded as it was by an affordable hotel, a restaurant, a staff housing tower and a cold beer and wine store, was in fact a literal home to generations of new arrivals in town. From the day it opened in 1967, the Ski Boot Motel was intended to be a warm and inclusive place. It may have been a few miles up the road from the ski lifts at the Southside, but for five bucks a night ski bums could afford to stay for weeks at a time and shuttle to and from the lifts in the motel's Purple People Eater bus. When the beer parlour opened in 1970, they also had somewhere to socialize at night, only a hop, skip and a stumble from their rooms. The Ski Boot was a self-sufficient resort that thrived on inclusiveness. When the power went out in the rest of the valley, its propane system kept many a local warm. And with its rough-and-tumble decor, cheap beer and for many years the only pool table in town, the beer parlour became a favourite local hangout. Later dubbed the Locals' Living Room, the feeling of home at the Boot ran deep. To its staff and many of its patrons, it was the hearth at the centre of things.

Like any good pub, the Boot's across-the-board hospitality extended beyond patrons of the human variety. Bob Brant, owner and manager of the Boot with his family in the eighties once asked, "Where else could you ride a horse into the bar?" There were usually up to half-a-dozen dogs hanging out in the pub, waiting patiently to escort their masters home, not to mention a resident cat named T.C. and some short-lived visits from a chicken with a penchant for rum and Coke. I sat down with three Boot, Shoestring Lodge and Gaitors Restaurant stalwarts who had fearlessly guided the establishment through its final fifteen years of life. Aussie Paul "Knuckles" McNaught, Janine "J-9" Jeffrey, Mike "Coco" Walsh and I took a table upstairs at Citta'. As the afternoon wore on and many pitchers of beer went down, more and more displaced Boot patrons joined the table and added their memories to the mix.

Janine was the heart and soul of the Boot Pub for its last decade and a half—dubbed the Mother Superior by some—with her Cheshire cat grin and boisterous, room-wide laugh emanating from behind her bar. Her cat T.C.—short for Tower Cat after the staff housing wing where they shared a room—wasn't afraid of much, and could sometimes be found in the mosh pit on Sunday punk nights. "That's what I loved," Janine said. "When the dogs and cats could get along. And when people would fight, I mean, if my dog and cat can get along, why are you guys arguing over free pool?" On occasion it was necessary to kick the canines out of the pub, such as one case that involved Mr. Coffee, beloved member of the Whistler community, and his doggie sidekick. "No problem when it's just quiet time," Janine said, "but when the strippers start it's really loud music and idiots looking at tits, not the floor, so they'd step on the dog. And so I was asking Mr. Coffee to take the dog out, and he was going, 'No, it's okay.' And I'm going, 'No, it's a dog. You've got to take it out.' And he goes, 'No, it's a girl!'" And nineteen too, I presume.

While the animals generally got along while sharing floor space in the Locals' Living Room, the humans didn't always co-exist in such harmony. Janine remembers a brawl breaking out one night when a bunch of young guys from Vancouver who were in town working on a construction job came in "to get into some shit." If they were looking for trouble, they didn't even have to leave the room. In the melee Janine's serving tray was knocked out of her hands. "This guy knocked into it, and instead of trying to catch it I just let it go, because I knew I'd hurt myself trying to catch glass. Then all of a sudden, 'Whoom.' One guy, we think he 'tripped,' but his face bashed into the pool table corner pocket. These guys who wanted to start some chaos ended up getting airlifted outta here."

As my friend Bosco Colebrook pointed out in the piece he wrote for the *Answer* about another incident at the Boot, "To qualify for barroom brawl status a fracas has to include everyone in the bar, although it is not absolutely essential for the majority of the combatants to know how the melee started." This particular one qualified not only on that count, but had the added bonus of including members of the Vancouver Canucks hockey team, no strangers to dropping the gloves for an occasional fight.

Working as a liftee on Whistler Mountain at the time, Bosco had been given the task earlier in the day of showing some of the Canucks around the mountain. Thus he'd had the good fortune of already befriending the three, Harold Snepsts, Ron Sedlbauer and Kenny Lockett, who were sitting at a table next to a group of Squamish bikers called the Tribesmen.

"Well, I was the one who started it," Bosco proclaimed

proudly. "Three of them were there and one of them went to sleaze a game of pool. I was really corked, eh, and as he was racking the balls, I whapped him across the knuckles with the fucking pool cue. And he got rather agitated with that." The biker traded some heated words with Bosco before sitting back down with his buddies. "They were planning all kinds of horse-shit, right. They were obviously going to get me," he said. The bikers were also doing their best to irritate the three Canucks, whose team had recently been knocked out of the first round of the playoffs by the Montreal Canadiens. Harold Snepsts, one of the toughest enforcers in the NHL at the time, walked up to the pool table to clarify matters with Bosco. "These guys are start-ing to really piss us off," he said. "If something happens we're not going to have to fight the whole bar, are we?" Bosco said, "No, I think you'd be doing everyone a favour." The moment Snepsts sat back down in his chair, one of the bikers leaned over the table and poured a beer over his head. "And that was

Boot Pub bartender and mother superior Janine (J-9) Jeffrey spends some time on the other side of the bar with friends Alison Williams (left) and Jen Jackson (centre). PHOTO CHRIS WOODALL

it," Bosco said. "That was all you needed. The fucking fists were flying." Bosco described the ensuing brawl in the *Answer*:

They say that the hand is quicker than the eye. The Canucks swarmed the bikers, with tables and chairs strewn in their wake. Now that the gloves were off, some very quick Canuck hands applied themselves to some slow Tribesmen eyes.

At the start of the ruckus the positions were easily defined. Three against three, one table versus the other. But like chess, once the battle is engaged, an almost infinite amount of following moves present themselves. Flailing bodies quickly spread out from the vortex. As the field of battle expanded, so did the participation level. As tables would get knocked over there was little else for the people sitting at them to do but jump up and join the fray. Very quickly the entire bar was engulfed as a result of this domino effect.

It would be difficult to tell what exactly happened without the benefit of a slow motion replay—suffice to say that Don Cherry would've been frothing at the mouth. One highlight clearly visible, and audible, was Snepsts lifting a biker about a foot off the floor with a sizzling uppercut.

What the newcomers were fighting about, however, and whom they were fighting, is still a mystery. The prevailing theory is that you attack randomly, operating on the assumption that anyone close enough to attack is just about to assault you. There is little doubt that some skirmishes were going on between combatants who were, two minutes previous, enjoying a beer together.

In the main event, the Canucks clearly TKO'ed the bikers. In the satellite bouts, it's anybody's guess. It was all over in under three minutes, when there were no chairs and tables to tip over.

The police were an hour away in Squamish in those days, Bosco said, and once the bikers unceremoniously left the bar, the owner showed up and kicked them out of their hotel room as well. Ten minutes after the fight, with the furniture all back in place, there was no sign that anything out of the ordinary had taken place, apart from some nursed cuts and bruises. On his way out at the end of the night, Ron Sedlbauer reportedly remarked to the bartender, "That was the weirdest thing. Guys were just jumping in for practice."

Years later, Bosco was sitting in the dentist's chair when he discovered that the dentist working on him also worked on the remaining teeth of the Vancouver Canucks players. When he learned that Bosco had written the story in the *Answer* about the Boot brawl, he said, "No way, you wrote that? They've got that story framed on the wall in their dressing room."

But apart from the odd barroom brawl, the Boot offered a welcoming room with an easygoing vibe. "It was a great place," Janine said. "We didn't have much of an après, but we sure had a lot of good local yokels. People who would be staying at the Chateau would go 'Where do the locals hang out?' and they'd find the Boot. Even though they were spending huge money there, they'd drink at our bar. From all over the world. They went, 'This is the kind of place where we drink at home.'"

One of the locals that visitors to the Boot likely would have found there in the afternoon was Seppo Makinen. Seppo left his mark in the valley not only with the many ski runs he cut on Whistler Mountain, one of which bears his name, but with his routine of afternoon patio-crawls that took him through the village to his final stop at the Boot before heading home to his house on Nesters Road. He was a fixture on Whistler's patios, easily identifiable with his broad, lumberman's build, a smile on his square jaw and bright eyes beneath a greying brush cut. I would occasionally have a beer with him when our paths crossed and listen to his wealth of stories while trying to sift the English from the Finnish. The Reverend Mike Varrin, director of bars at Whistler Blackcomb, once performed a tribute to Seppo in which he lovingly mimicked his accent gradually morphing from understandable English to 90 percent Finnish as his afternoon circuit wore on.

Janine outlined Seppo's regular flight plan: "He'd start at Tapley's, Citta', the Longhorn, Merlin's, Monk's and then the Boot. And that was his little trail home. He'd stop at the Boot to see the boobies, and then he'd crawl home. He always kept his straws to know how many drinks he had. Bacardi and Coke. And he'd go, 'Oh, I've had five.' Once he got to six he'd leave." Seppo began building his sprawling log home on Nesters Road just south of the Boot back in the late sixties. It was the site of some great parties over the years with its many rooms, pool table, hot tub built into the basement rocks and outdoor swimming pool. He later operated it as an informal hostel, and many young people who arrived in town spent their first Whistler nights there if they couldn't get a room at the Ski Boot. Chances were they'd run into Seppo at the Boot after skiing and he'd told them about his place just up the road. And if they didn't have the cash, it was likely they were welcome just the same. "I stayed there once for two weeks when I was a little destitute," Janine remembered, "and he didn't charge me anything because I had the bottom room and it was flooded. He had a pair of rubber boots for me there, but the bed was on an uplift, and I'm with all the tools and shit."

The old wooden structure went up in flames in April 1998. "When the fire happened, he was more worried about everybody else," Janine said. "He lost everything he had, all his memories, everything, and he was worried about the kids who lost a toothbrush. When we offered him that room to stay at the Shoestring for free for a couple of months, he goes, 'No, give it

to one of these guys.' He was just proud, a proud, proud man."
After his house burnt down, Seppo lived in his trailer in Lot 4,
a short walk up Blackcomb Way toward the village. Ron Ross
and another friend found him there a few days after his final
walk home from the Boot in November 1999. He'd fallen and
hit his head on the counter in the cold trailer where he hadn't
even had a chance to turn on the propane heat. Paul McNaught
was manager of the Boot at the time. "Yeah, it's a shame that no
one could rally together at the end," he said, "when his health
went down, and he was in a trailer. You know, he was such an
icon." After Seppo passed away, Janine says, a group of friends
hosted the annual Seppo Walk that followed his regular patio
route through the village and back to the Boot.

Seppo and Ron were good friends and co-owners of a property across the highway from Mons. Ron was also the owner of
the rum-and-Coke-drinking chicken that frequented the Boot
for a short time. Someone
from Maple Ridge had given
it to him one day, and when
he got back to Whistler he
brought it along to the pub.
"The dog, the cat and the
chicken got along," Janine
said, breaking into a laugh.
Paul was managing the bar
during the time of the chick-
en's visits. "I walk in the back
door, and I'm looking at it,"
he said, his Australian accent
beginning to thicken a little as
our afternoon wore on. "I'm
going, 'There's a chicken sitting on the table?' I thought it

Ski run logger and local character
Seppo Makinen displays a
characteristic smile and a raised half-
pint. PHOTO COURTESY PAUL FOURNIER

was a remote control [animal]. I was looking at it and it was going like this [mimes chicken bobbing its head]. And I'm going, 'Are you serious, is it real?' Everyone's laughing at me, and I go, 'Great. Cats. Dogs. Chickens now.' I really thought it was a remote control and someone was having a go at me." Like many others who took a shine to the Boot, that chicken became a regular at the picnic table in front of the bar, where it discovered its affinity for its drink of choice. One night after leaving the bar, already well into its cups, the chicken came to a bad end and fell easy prey to a prowling coyote.

Paul first came to the Boot as a young arrival in town looking for a cheap place to stay. He and five friends got a room at the Shoestring, and after partying to excess at the Boot's ninety-nine-cent Monday beer night, they managed to get kicked out of their hotel room. "It was minus twenty," he said, "and being Australian, you know, we're not used to this weather, so I got on my knees and teared up." Paul's performance not only kept a roof over their heads, but shortly thereafter landed him a job. He started working as the maintenance man, which at the Boot proved to be a kind of perpetual employment program. "You know, I set the Boot Pub on fire, jackhammering through a tequila line. A spark came up and the tequila caught fire. It was when we were taking the carpet out and putting a wood floor down. So we had a jug of tequila . . . at three in the morning."

Another one of Paul's construction projects resulted in melting the hotel lobby. The little glassed-in entranceway to the lobby had a wood floor that was being changed over to tile. "It was the middle of winter," Paul remembered, "and I had to keep the plywood dry as skiers were coming in and out, so I got the biggest, burliest heater from Sabre [Rentals], put it in there and fired it up. I went down to the workshop, and two minutes later I'm coming back up and everyone's screaming. I walk in there and I go, 'Eeeeaaahhh!' like I can't breath. Turn it off. When the mist or whatever, the fog rests, every telephone, everything that was plastic melted. Like, the telephone receivers were two feet long. And I had to call Caroline, my boss. I for sure thought I was fired. I meet her in the car park and I go, 'It's not good. It's not good at all.' And when she walked in she just laughed . . . So I got to keep my job there."

Paul ended up working at almost every job the Shoestring Lodge and Boot Pub had to offer, from bartending to DJing for the strippers, to waitering and managing the restaurant. He shared a room in the hotel with his girlfriend, Tammy Alain, who managed the Boot Pub for three years. Their dog, Kai, was a fixture on the premises. "Kai lived at the Boot for twelve years with us. He was a husky–shepherd–wolf," Paul said. "Kai brought up my cat," Janine interjected. "He was like the mascot," Paul said. "There was an evening where it started to get busy in the Boot and there were seven dogs in there, and it was time to kick every dog out. And no dog was happy about being kicked out. It's Wednesday night, prime rib. Well, I had a doorman and he just started moving them. And Kai refused to leave and this little doorman Tim, he just pointed at Kai at the very end and he goes, 'You, out.' And Kai got himself up and just looked at him, shook his head at the doorman like, 'I'm the son of the boss, and you're kicking me out?' And then he walked out with his tail between his legs."

Perhaps inspired by Seppo's patio crawls, Kai would also sometimes tour the village establishments. "I used to get phone calls from Citta' too," Paul recalled. "'Paul, your dog's here.' I'd ask them, 'Can you put him in a cab?' The cabs would take him to the Boot, and I'd just pay the bill when he got here."

Like most good hotel pubs, the Boot also provided refuge for its resident ghosts. "Yeah, there was a ghost there for sure," Mike said. "And I don't believe in ghosts." At the end of one evening, around 2:30 or 3:00 in the morning, Tammy, Paul and Mike were at the bar having their "after sipper," Paul's Aussie term for an after-work drink. "Now, I was standing behind the bar, and Tammy and Coco were sitting facing the bar, and the women's washroom door opened up and the light shined. That's why I just went, 'Wow!' and then it closed. It's a heavy door, a heavy wood door. We have left people in the bar before, and I thought for sure someone was unconscious in there. Anyway, I went around the bar and I started walking to the door. Coco was behind me and he's got his hands on my back, just kind of freaking out. I get to the door and I kick it in and go, 'Who's there?' and no one's there. No one at all was there . . . We'd been told stories about the ghost, but this was a legitimate story. I was like, 'Well, it's obviously a chick ghost cause she's in the females'. So we left it at that, but at the end of the night we promised not to tell anyone because they all thought we'd be high on something."

Like many staffers at the Boot and Shoestring Lodge, Mike

Paul "Knuckles" McNaught (left) and Tim Staritt man the Boot bar where a photo of the late Seppo Makinen hangs above. PHOTO COURTESY JEN JACKSON AND ROB HUGHES

lived for a time in the Tower, which jutted above the restaurant and housed nine rooms and a communal kitchen for staff. "I lasted a month," he said. Janine recalled the motto that accompanied life in the Tower: "'What happens in the Tower, stays in the Tower!' Our nickname was the Tower Dwellers." Paul only lasted two days in the Tower before moving into a room in the Shoestring, but Janine lived there happily for over a decade. "I didn't realize how important sleep was until I moved out, thirteen years later," she said, bursting into one of her hearty laughs. "The best thing about the Tower," Paul added, "was all the staff were up there, so you could always keep an eye on them. If they weren't at work, or were late for work, you knew where they were."

Paul managed Gaitors, the restaurant upstairs, for four years. When he decided to return to Australia forever, Mike took over managing the restaurant. But Paul's forever turned out to be less than a month: he was back in Whistler in twenty-nine days. "I came back and then I asked Coco for a job, because he had my job now. Within twenty-nine days he was my boss," Paul said. "And he put me on weekend breakfasts. He knows I'm not good in the morning." Gaitors was a favourite dinner place for locals and especially young Whistler families. It had a laid-back atmosphere, a wooden plank floor, a window view of Whistler and Blackcomb and good Mexican food at very reasonable prices. The beautiful wooden bar off to one side created a circular route for the kids to run around while their parents dug into their fajitas and margaritas. Paul then took over managing the pub and immediately implemented a strict code for selecting new staff. "My hiring technique was, 'Do you drink and do you smoke weed? No? Well, are you prepared to take it up?'"

At that time the Boot was famous for its low-priced drinks. There were ninety-nine-cent beer nights and, while Tammy was still managing, experiments with ninety-nine-cent shooter nights. Perhaps thinking they'd be safe at a distance, Paul and Tammy went on vacation to Mexico when the first ninety-nine-cent Friday shooters went down. "So everyone else had to look after it," Paul remembered. "We phoned them two days after that Friday in Mexico and said, 'How many shooters did you sell?' It was 5000 and something. 'And how many did you spill?' We lost a nickel on each one." The shooter experiment took place during the bar wars in Whistler, and the other establishments in town were not happy with the Boot's specials. Paul had to attend meetings of the newly formed bar and restaurant association, Food and Beverage Whistler, along with all the other bar managers and the liquor inspector—a dicey proposition for an Australian illegal alien managing the Locals' Living Room. The upshot of the meetings was that the Boot agreed to up their special beer price to $1.25, which resulted in a 25 percent increase in profits and much happier bartenders, who now would get between 25 and 75 cents for tips instead of a penny.

The Boot had regular Sunday Punk Night and Monday Night Madness with live music and cheap drinks, but it was a comfortable place to hang out anytime. Tim Staritt bartended there for many years alongside Ted Tempany. He recently told me, "It was a place you didn't have to think about going out to. It didn't matter what you were wearing, it was like walking into your living room. You didn't need to plan to go out to the Boot." And for many people in town, the Boot Pub became the nexus for a kind of extended family. Tanya Clark, the other T.C., who waitressed there for six years, put it this way: "I'd come out to Whistler for a year, and was going to go back to Ontario. I didn't feel all that connected to the place, but then I met all these people through the Boot, and it really was like my family. I've been here for sixteen years now."

Jen Jackson and Rob "Cat" Hughes found a similar sense of family at the Boot. For the last few years when it was known that the Boot was slated for destruction, Jen and Rob had a standing offer when they'd walk in the door. Janine or Paul would say, "Two ice cold beers, first one's on us." Their dog, Jack-Straw, was known to go up to the bar on his hind legs, say "Hi" to Janine and order a bowl of popcorn. "We booked the whole Boot with She Stole My Beer for our fifth anniversary," Jen said, as she and Rob joined us in progress upstairs at Citta', "because we knew we weren't going to be spending our tenth anniversary there. And we asked everybody to put some money in the donation box at the door. We were taking a bit of a risk. We were paying the band and we were providing all of the party favours. So at the end of the night we were up in the office counting all the five-dollar bills and we came up to $2300. And we filled the room for the night with all of our friends."

Brian Walker, once a bar manager himself in Hamilton, Ontario, joined us to share some of his own Boot memories. "There was a head table," he said, "It was the brain trust of the Boot. The table right up at the front, and sometimes as soon as it would open up in the afternoon there would be a gathering of people there and it would last on into the evening. I don't know how many times I found somebody at the table who'd take over the pool table with me for the rest of the evening. Ruling the pool table at the Boot was a badge of honour. The land mine you had to negotiate to win a game on that table. It was ill lit, I don't think there was any kind of lighting over the thing whatsoever, the worst table to shoot on. It had rolls, you would never ever want to finesse a shot into a pocket, not a chance." "Home court advantage," Jen quipped. "That's part of the charm," Janine added. "I remember, just before the Boot closed down," Brian continued. "Princess Stephanie [Reesor] was there and she surfed

Regular Boot patron Jack-Straw eyes a pint of lager while ordering his bowl of popcorn from Janine at the bar. PHOTO COURTESY JEN JACKSON AND ROB HUGHES

that pool table out the door. The guys had it up on a lift and Stephanie was posed up there riding it out the door."

Jordan White, another member of the Boot's extended family, wandered upstairs from his seat at the Citta' bar. Jordan is a longtime local and wizard of the Hammond B-3 organ with much-loved West Vancouver–Whistler band, She Stole My Beer. "Well, initially it was the only place we could play," Jordan said of the band's early days at the Boot, "so it provided accessibility. It also provided security on many levels: on a friendship level because I had friends working there; and on a security level once again it provided income, sustainability. After we did it for a long time, it provided a sort of reinforcement, because as you'd return it was a reaffirmation of what you were doing, and that made you feel good."

Beyond playing there as a band member, Jordan said, the Boot made an impression on a personal level: "It was a home, it provided many things that a family would provide: company, reinforcement, encouragement. And then at the very end of the day, it was just something that you would seek out once you got sick of the fuckin' rigmarole in the village. As Whistler progressed, you'd always go back to the Boot to look for the thing that initially attracted you to this place."

Many bands found that sense of hominess at the Boot, from just-arrived young musicians at the Sunday- or Thursday-night jams to touring bands from across Canada and North America. In the early nineties, then-Whistler-based photographer and writer Chris Woodall began photographing all the bands that played the Boot and displaying the black-and-white photographs on the Wall of Fame inside the pub. The Wall soon extended around most of the room and included photos of Carol Pope, DOA, the Smalls, King Apparatus, Sonny Rhodes, Curious George, SNFU, Garaj Mahal, She Stole My Beer, Day Glow Abortions, the Rheostatics, the Hounds of Buskerville, Slow Nerve Action and dozens of other bands who played the small room that was capable of holding only 125 people legally. The Boot was a good stopover on a tour leaving Vancouver and a chance for bands to experience a down-home venue—the last thing they would have expected in Whistler.

The biggest coup for the Boot pub was undoubtedly when the Tragically Hip came to town. The band was already familiar with Whistler, having played at Buffalo Bills in the early nineties when they were a little-known up-and-comer. By the time the Hip played the Boot in 2002, they were international rock stars more accustomed to playing stadiums. Getting them on stage didn't take any bold initiative or clever strategizing, Paul remembered. "They actually booked me, I didn't book them, if anyone wants to know. What happened was they phoned me and I hung up on 'em, because I thought it was a trick phone call. Mark Friedman, I think his name was, the manager of the band, said they were in town and wanted to play at the Boot Pub. And I hung up. Anyway, he calls back again and I stayed on the line. Then I realized, gee, they are in town. They're staying at Nicklaus North and they're writing half their album there."

It was finally confirmed that the Hip would play two nights that fall at the Boot Pub. The band wanted to donate the proceeds to a charity and since the first bear of the season had recently been shot, Paul decided to name the Jennifer Jones Bear Society and the Whistler Food Bank as the recipients. The plan was to be kept secret until shortly before the shows. Then, after a drought-plagued summer, the fall rains hit Whistler and the Sea-to-Sky area with tragic force. In the early morning hours of October 18, the Rutherford Creek Bridge between Whistler and Pemberton washed out in a torrential flood. Two staff members from the Boot Pub, Darryl Stevenson and Michael Benoit, and three from Moe Joes nightclub in the village, Jamie and Casey Burnette and Ed Elliot, were driving home after work to Pemberton when their vehicles plunged into the river. Casey Burnette was the only survivor.

The loss of the young men shook the community and especially their co-workers at the two establishments. Andy Flynn, owner of Moe Joe's, hosted a fundraising concert for the victims' families and an account was set up at the Royal Bank—Jamie Burnette was newly married and the father of a four-month-old son. Paul still couldn't let on that the Tragically Hip was slated to play at the Boot, but he rearranged the plans so that the families would also benefit from the concerts. "I always get a shiver when I talk about that," he said of the Rutherford Creek tragedy. "I called the management of the Hip and I asked them—because they only wanted to charge a ten-dollar ticket—and I told them about the tragedy and I said, "Can we up the price to twenty dollars and we'll put it to the victims of the Rutherford Bridge?" That's where it was set in motion."

Selling the tickets was clearly not going to be a problem, but circulating them fairly among fans in the community was the challenge. "I was the most popular man in Whistler for forty-eight hours," Paul said. "I only let on thirty-six hours before the Tuesday- and Wednesday-night shows." He called the bar managers and other hospitality operators in town and gave them each ten names for the guest list on each night. "Yeah, for two nights, with a 125-capacity bar we had 332 in the first night and 337 in the second night. I got three citations, and I was in well with the liquor inspector, and she let us off. I just said to her, 'We raised $17,000.' I was blown away because they're my favourite Canadian band, for sure. And you know, the band came up to Coco's restaurant and sat with the victims' families and friends."

The Soul Shakedown

The next big event at the Boot was undoubtedly the pub's closing party. The directors of Cressey, the company that owned the property, met early in 2006 with Paul, Mike and Geoff "Effie" MacDonald, who was managing the hotel. Redevelopment plans had been in the works for some years, and had finally been given approval from Whistler council. After getting a firm closing date so the staff would know where they stood with their jobs, Paul asked the directors, "So, what do you want to do? Are we gonna have a shindig?" Jen Jackson coined the name Soul Shakedown as she emerged one night from the Boot's brain trust at table one. It not only carried the double entendre of the boot's sole and the soul of the Boot, but had the ring of a good shaker.

The Whistler Museum and Archives Society was well aware of the special place the Boot held in Whistler's collective imagination, and it began working with the Boot management to preserve what it could, and to turn the closing party into a fundraiser for the society. One idea involved people taking home a piece of the Boot in the form of a shake from the roof in exchange for a donation. "I had people come in and ask me to sign the shingles," Janine remembered. "I felt so Paris Hilton. I'm famous. I've done nothing but I'm famous." She added, "My biggest concern when the Boot died was where are the young 'uns going to start out? It really broke my heart. And you wouldn't believe how many kids had been told by their aunties and uncles, 'When you go to Whistler, say hey to J-9 or Paul.' It was the coolest thing. And now you have respect from these kids."

The collection of classic ski boots from different eras that had adorned the high shelves in the pub since 1970 were slated to go to the museum, though not everything went according to plan during the final weeks at the Boot. "We took a lot of stuff out of there for the Museum and Archives before it was wrecked," Paul recalled. The wreckage began early—long before the official demolition crew showed up—on the final Punk night. Three Inches of Blood was playing and toward the end of the night, the rambunctious crowd began to tear things like shelving and pictures from the walls. "It was heart-breaking," Janine said of the shape they left her bar in. "And then those little monkeys didn't come down to see how the humans take 'er out." Paul came down earlier in the evening to check on things. "I was in my office, hiding," he joked. "I went down there just to check on it and I see all the doormen covered in blood. And I'd had a few drinks, but it was actually dried blood [paint] they'd painted all over themselves. I decided to do one last stage dive off the stage into the crowd, and I got pummeled, kicked and trodden and stepped on. I picked myself up, walked back out through the lobby and back up to my office, back on the couch and thought, 'God, I didn't deserve that.'"

The pub was put back together well enough for Friday night's unofficial closing party with She Stole My Beer. The evening had the same happy vibe and camaraderie of any She Stole My Beer show, but was tinged with the gravity of saying goodbye to a historic and much-loved watering hole. The pub was filled with hundreds of locals, Peggy and I among them, and was still packed well past closing time as the band played on into the wee hours.

First thing in the morning Paul had to meet with the RCMP to make sure everything was in order for the thousands of people expected at Saturday's outdoor Soul Shakedown. "It must have been blowing eighty knots sou'east," Paul recalled, "pouring rain. And we have the chief of police walking around with me at eight o'clock in the morning with my sunglasses on. He goes, 'Paul, why are your sunglasses on?' I lifted them and my eyes are bleeding from being up for four days, and he goes, 'Put 'em back on.' I said, 'So, you happy with everything?' And he goes, 'Yup, we'll be checking back later.'"

There was still an enormous amount of preparation work to do for the party, Paul remembered, and nobody else showed up in the morning. "You know what, it was a bloody hard effort to get that place closed under the supervision of delinquents," he said, not entirely excluding himself from the judgment. "Cressey offered no rewards, no severance or anything like that, so it was really hard to keep staff involved." Along with the staff who eventually did show up, Paul called in the help of good friends. "Jen and Rob 'Cat' were rock stars," he said. "I called them in early, and I had Rob dig a ditch." Rob recalled the effort to bury the cables from the hotel to the stage: "It was about a foot deep and forty feet long, but I was hungover, and it pretty near killed me." Jen and others helped staff set up and run the bar in the beer garden. "We worked for like eight hours," she said. "We were doing serious double time."

By early afternoon things were roughly in place and Paul

went up to his office for a brief nap before the multitudes arrived. "I was just absolutely tired and I fell asleep on the couch. My little brother called me from Australia, and he said, 'How's it going?' And all of a sudden the sun came through my office window and I woke up, and I look out. I think I was asleep for twenty minutes, and I looked outside, there's five hundred more people in there. We were expecting about 5000 people, we got about 2500 that came."

For my part, I'd already celebrated the Boot's closing the night before and had gotten up early to take my son Jonathan to a soccer game in Pemberton. I stopped in Saturday afternoon just to get rid of the two tickets we had for the event. I'd found buyers and started walking away down the Valley Trail when the sun burned through the clouds. Perhaps it was the same moment that Paul's brother phoned from Australia. Suddenly it seemed imperative that I not miss this final farewell to one of Whistler's most venerable institutions. Before I knew it, I was inside the fence with all the other revellers.

And what a party it was. While Friday night had attracted a loyal group of Boot patrons and She Stole My Beer fans, here was the whole cross-section of the community arrayed on the grass and volleyball courts next to Fitzsimmons Creek. Everyone from Charlie Doyle and Kashi and Bob Daniels to Ed Gordon, Mark Schnaidt, Nancy Wilhelm-Morden, Mark MacLaurin, Ace Mackay-Smith and hundreds of other full- and part-time Whistlerites I'd gotten to know over the last thirty years, not to mention innumerable kids, dogs and one brave punk-rock cat named T.C. Over a quarter of Whistler's population was out to say their farewell to a piece of valley history. The museum set up a video camera inside the Boot Pub where people could record their favourite Boot stories, do a pole dance and buy a roofing shake signed, if they liked, by the famous Janine. Local band A Whole Lotta Led played on the big outdoor stage in the afternoon before Vancouver's Soulstream took over for the final set.

As the afternoon wore on, feet started moving and mouths started wagging as old, well-heeled locals traded their favourite Boot stories and memories in the beer garden. The growing lineups for beer just created more time to catch up with old friends. Jen Jackson remembered the scene from the other side of the bar. "That was one of the great things," she said. "Right in the full prime time of the bar area, there had to have been like seven, eight deep of people wanting beer. All of a sudden Dave Highway said, 'Okay, people, we've been running off of our asses for three hours straight, everyone to the back, safety meeting.' We all drank a beer, smoked a cigarette, smoked whatever, watching the lineup get bigger and bigger. For five minutes. Like, come on, we're working for free here." I think I was standing in the lineup right about then, and perhaps it was the lull in pouring that led me to grab a pen and scrawl down a few words about the Boot's demise on a napkin before stuffing it in my pocket.

As the sun went down, Soulstream took the stage with former Whistlerite Karen Graves on saxophone, clarinet and vocals. Karen used to come out to the Sunday jazz nights at the Highland Lodge and has since become a successful jazz musician and composer based out of Vancouver who also plays with some of the city's hottest funk and R & B bands. That night she was just another member of the community saying her goodbye to the Boot and reacquainting herself with long-time friends.

At nightfall, Paul pulled out the Soul Shakedown surprise finale. "I just went to the fire department and said, 'Can I have fireworks?' And they said, 'Sure, Paul.'" Astounded that he didn't have to sign forms and fill out endless applications, he purchased five minutes' worth of pyrotechnics that ran the

Cressey party bill up another $3000. When it came time to set them off, there were cars parked too close to the designated launch pad. "There were some vehicles sitting in the top lot that we kept pulling out, and announcing, 'Move your vehicles, move your vehicles,' and then it was like too late. Let 'em rip. We burnt the roofs of three cars, the tops of their roofs," Paul confessed.

The place emptied quickly after the fireworks finished and people started wandering home or heading elsewhere to continue their Saturday-night festivities. I was ready to call it quits, and started walking to the highway to catch a bus home. On my shortcut through the Shoestring Lodge, something drew me upstairs to take one last look at Gaitors Restaurant. Twenty-five or thirty people were seated around the wooden bar and the adjacent alcove enjoying the warm ambience of the place one last time. Nobody seemed to be manning the ship, so I went behind the bar and cracked a beer. A few more people wandered in and wanted to order drinks as well. I must have looked convincingly like a bartender because before I knew it I was serving drinks like I'd been working there my whole life. No more sneaking cases of Canadian out to the rock behind the pub with my teenage friends: I'd finally made it to the controls at the epicentre of the Boot. More than a few people commented on the great work I was doing, pleased too I'm sure by the fact that the drinks were all free. After I put in a solid shift, other patrons began to catch on and more were ready to take over whenever the last volunteer needed a break.

"My friends who came out from Ontario for that final party," Mike recalled, "they were going down to the beer and wine store and buying booze, and coming back up and selling it because there was no booze left." By that time I was already on my way home, with a glass of brandy in one hand and one of Gaitors' purple wooden chairs in the other, a memento of

Whistler history that now sits around my dining table next to my salvaged Dusty's chair. I crossed the highway and waited for my bus at Nesters, wise enough when it arrived to leave the brandy glass behind. The bus driver deemed that the chair was okay to bring along. "Just keep it out of the aisle," he warned.

The Boot Pub and Shoestring Lodge didn't give up their ghosts easily. Even the living continued to occupy the establishment for some time after the Soul Shakedown. "We protected it for about forty-eight hours, the whole building, " Paul said. "Actually, we were still down at the volleyball courts [the next day] when they removed the tents. All the couches from the lobby were down there, so . . . they just lifted the tent right off us, then we moved back into the building." That's when Paul discovered that someone had changed the design of the Shoestring Lodge to a more open floor plan. No one has ever owned up to the architectural redesign, but it was now possible to look all the way to the end of the wing from the first room. "I could see right through the walls . . . Someone had literally punched their way through each drywall. And I go, 'Ah no. Are we going to get any bonus out of this?'"

Upstairs at Gaitors, things weren't looking much better. Mike had gone home at some point to get some sleep. "I brought him back in and he walked in and he cried," Paul said. Mike laughed about it, remembering how they got down to cleaning up, putting things back together as best they could. "A lot of stuff that we cleaned up and put aside and boxed up for Cressey, it took a lot of time, and then they just left it all there and people started breaking in. The next thing you know, the $25,000 computer system was gone." Mike had asked the owners if he could salvage the wooden bar and plank flooring, but after the fire department was given the go ahead to use it for practice, the restaurant was submerged in a foot of water and anything of value was ruined.

Janine remembered her last walk through the place. "I'm going, 'I really don't want to go in to the Shoestring because it's going to break my heart.' We went up through Gaitors and that's when I saw all the devastation, of the wood and the bar and the computer smashed, everything smashed. We're walking down and it's dark because all the boarded windows. And with all the squatters that were there, it wasn't as bad as I thought." The Ski Boot Hotel, originally built to house ski bums, was turned back over to them for its final weeks. "Well," Paul said, putting it into perspective, "somebody needed a place to live." As for the Soul Shakedown, Paul concluded, "I can honestly say I don't think I'd do it any differently. I just remember waking up one day in a bed, and I was at home, and Coco's wife was calling Coco. I thought I was still in the Shoestring Lodge because I just lived like six days at the Shoestring to get the final Shakedown complete, you know. It was a hell of an effort, that's for sure."

As for me, I woke up the morning after the Boot's closing party and sat down at the kitchen table on my new Gaitors chair

Nearly forty years of beer-soaked history at the Boot and Shoestring Lodge was flushed away with the first wrecking ball hit. PHOTO DAVE STEERS

for some breakfast. When I reached into my pocket I found a napkin on which somebody had scrawled a beer garden haiku:

Boot Pub's going down
My beer is nearly empty
The town's footwear, gone

9

Spring Thaw

At the end of the ski season in a mountain town, certain rituals are re-enacted every year. The après patio activity reaches its peak not only because the days are growing longer, but because the snow that justifies its existence is rapidly melting. Spring is all about slush and slushy drinks. Back in the seventies, the official shift from winter season to off-season occurred on the May 24 long weekend. All manner of mayhem was unleashed on the valley in honour of Queen Victoria who bestowed such a timely holiday upon the ski bums. These could include a freestyle or hotdogging contest on Whistler Mountain, a gelandesprung contest, the Great Snow Earth Water Race, belly-flop and wet T-shirt contests, live bands and beer gardens.

The Great Snow Earth Water Race was perhaps the truest homage to the disappearing white stuff. Each five-person relay team included a skier, a cyclist, two canoeists and a runner. The skiers congregated in a mass at the foot of the Ridge Run with their skis parked in another mass near the top of the Red Chair. The Le Mans start began with a sprint for the boards, followed by an all-out inferno race to the bottom of the mountain. On May 24, the snow line is liable to sit anywhere from above midstation on Whistler's southside to the valley bottom. It can also sneak up on unsuspecting racers by waiting behind a knoll or just around a south-facing corner in the form of suddenly exposed mud, rock and bushes. In the places where the snow ends, the race turns into a mad dash of accelerated running, sliding and cartwheeling to the valley bottom.

The year my brother did the skiing leg of the Great Race he came down off the mountain in second place, freshly coated in mud and unrecognizable to everyone including his bike-riding teammate, Steve Morrison. (He was also unable to descend stairs forwards for an entire week.) Once the baton was passed on to Steve, he shot away on his ten-speed and managed to pass the one rider ahead of him. But when he got to the bottom of Lorimer Road, he missed the turnoff to the river and careened off into the forest. The comedy of errors continued when, sitting in fourth place, he passed the baton on to the two girls set to paddle part of the River of Golden Dreams and the length of Alta Lake. From a team perspective, it was unfortunate that the girls had never sat in a canoe before and were unaware that the adjective "tippy" often accompanies "canoe." They flipped the boat within the first few seconds, and then managed to zigzag their way southwards. The snaking River of Golden Dreams presented them with countless opportunities to learn how to steer their craft, and by the time they crossed the lake and reached Wayside Park, runner and Whistler builder Nelo Busdon was a twitching mess of Italian sprinter muscles. Starting somewhere back of fiftieth position, he managed to pass a couple dozen runners and put the team back into the middle of the pack.

This typical Snow Earth Water Race team fiasco, like hundreds of others over the years, demonstrated the appropriate ritualistic approach to the race. It wasn't about winning so much as following the path of the melting snow crystals, from alpine slush to runoff mud, through lake and filtering river system, and finally to the beer garden where the water molecules were magically transformed into lager by the god of brewing himself, Dionysus—a true ski-town ritual honouring the cycle of life.

Ironically, the demise of the Great Race didn't result from a lack of interest, but from an upsurge in participation from earnest and overzealous racers. National level skiers, riders and runners formed ringer teams, and semi-professional entrants began showing up from around the world. For a couple of years, a Japanese TV network sent a crew to film a team that had earned the right to participate by winning a TV contest. The 442 Communications Regiment of the armed forces set up posts on the mountain and along the River of Golden Dreams, using the race as an opportunity for field communications practice. Once teams started training months in advance and showing up on race day in tight spandex suits, the fun was subsumed by serious competitiveness. By 1990 the burden of organization had become too great, and the race finally collapsed under the weight of its own success.

On the other end of the spectrum, the long weekend dubbed May Day Madness was getting too wild and out of hand for the neo-conservative eighties. Beer gardens and unchecked partying were frowned upon and replaced by events far less memorable but more befitting an aspiring world-class resort. Still, deep-seated ritual has a way of re-emerging as the times change, and it wasn't long before the irrepressible end-of-season celebrations were back.

By the nineties, wild and extreme living was back in vogue;

in fact it had been rediscovered as the most marketable tonic since snake oil. The difference this time around was that the extreme-lifestyle image was now connected to products: beer, cars, sunglasses, even ski resorts themselves. It was in this climate that the World Ski and Snowboard Festival evolved. The event began in 1996 with a variety of ski and snowboarding competitions and, taking the opposite trajectory of the Snow Earth Water Race, gradually morphed into a ten-day, end-of-season party.

Along with the sliding competitions, the festival now encompasses a free outdoor concert series, photography, film, fashion and multimedia contests, an art show, the Chairlift Review theatre, a dog parade and countless other events and parties. From the beginning it was heartily embraced by the business community, which was happy to see full hotel beds in mid-April and an influx of $20 million into the resort economy. Over the years the festival has also made an effort to connect more with the community at large. Many residents take part in the events and parties, and nobody complains about catching free afternoon concerts with Toots and the Maytals, the Black-Eyed Peas, Michael Franti, Buck 65 or any number of Canadian and international acts. There's a sense of momentum to the festival, and if you don't mind running into the ubiquitous showroom Pontiacs, Hummers and corporate swag tents littered throughout the village, it's kind of like the earlier end-of-season festivities, but with a lot of well-positioned product placement.

The most fun and spirited end-of-season celebration these last couple of years has been the Hotdoggin' Après Party hosted by Ace Mackay-Smith. Ace's party takes place on the Monday after the World Ski and Snowboard Festival, just as the big stages are being dismantled in the village and the corporate tents and banners are being folded up and shipped off to the

More, and sometimes less, than T-shirts got wet at the Christianna Inn's
May 24 wet T-shirt contests, spring 1977. PHOTO COURTESY *WHISTLER ANSWER*

Retro ski fashions rule the day at the end-of-season Hotdoggin' Après Party, April 2009 (l–r: Kristy Litchfield, Mariko Fuchihara, Sasha Kusz, and Sammy-the-dog, winner of the hot-dog-eating contest). PHOTO ANDY DITTRICH

next promotion. The Garibaldi Lift Company, with its patio adjacent to the last strip of spring snow at the base of Whistler Mountain, is the perfect venue for this celebration of tight suits, toques and tunes. The retro-styled event features ski ballet, hot-dog-eating and limbo competitions. Mostly though, it's a return to celebrating for no other reason than to have some fun and say "so long" to winter, a true Coast Mountain ritual with no designs on fuelling the economy. The DJs play for what little money the door brings in, any excess proceeds after paying the organizers are given to a charity and the prizes are all donated by small—and banner-free—local businesses.

"I missed all the fun and silly ski contests that Whistler used to hold," Ace told me after one Hotdoggin' party. "The Restaurant Races, Slush Cups, Bigfoot Races. Everything these days seems to be about big sponsors and big prize money and only pro athletes." Along with her fond memories of springs past in Whistler, Ace was steeped in an early ski-bum culture at Tod Mountain where her dad was general manager in the seventies. "My best ski memories as a kid were from spring skiing," she said. "Our Dad loved throwing events to get families and party people all together for fun. He launched 'Wonder Weekend,' which consisted of such events as an obstacle race, ski-jousting, gully races, and the bum jump. Everyone dressed up in costume too. At night there was a big party and me and my brothers liked looking in the window of the Bierstube and watching hippies hang from the wagon wheel lighting fixture and guzzle beers upside-down. So, all these great memories inspired me to bring back the 'silly.' After all, skiing is just sliding down snow on planks. Pretty silly in itself."

I booked the day off writing and attended this year's Hotdoggin' Party with bells on, partying like it was 1979 and even entering the ski-ballet contest. Together with moguls and aerials, ski ballet was once part of freestyle's holy trinity. It

involved short skis, long poles and lots of spinning and jumping on a smooth and shallow slope accompanied by music, ideally played on a Radio Shack Realistic sound system. In order to
be a contender in the overall freestyle standings, mogul skiers
and aerialists also had to compete in the ballet event. But while
aerials and moguls developed into Olympic sports and continued as part of the World Cup Freestyle circuit, ski ballet was
abandoned in the nineties to the slush pond of has-been skiing
disciplines. As a historic curiosity and season-ending comedy,
however, ballet skiing still reigns supreme.

Athletic ability and experience mattered less than attitude
and frame of mind in the ballet contest I entered. The six-inch-
deep slush turned almost every manoeuvre into a potential
comic disaster and the steep starting ramp left over from the Big
Air competition struck fear into every competitor's heart, a fear

mitigated only by the great
equalizing force of the slushy
drinks and many party favours
liberally circulating around
the GLC patio. Wowing the
judges with a spinning and
trick-filled (not to mention
hamstring-pulling) first run
that included a half pole-flip
head plant, I found myself in
the finals. I was unprepared
in every sense of the word for
a second run, so I opted for
one big S-turn, beer in hand,
which I chugged at the bottom
and threw over my shoulder
as I boldly yelled "Freestyle
forever!" It was more

The author performs the time-
honoured "outrigger" manoeuvre.
Pulled hamstrings are often not felt
until the day after the Hotdoggin'
Après Party. PHOTO ANDY DITTRICH

performance art than bal-
let run, and I was more than
happy with my third place fin
ish. Tim "The Mighty" Quinn
showed true old-school grace
in the deep slush with second place, and men's winner
Kevan "Kamikaze" Kobayashi
threw a series of three-
quarter-rotation pole flips and
an incredible ski release and
re-entry without stopping in
front of the screaming crowd.
Rob Boyd, who won the ski
ballet in 2008, was not in the
field, but rumour has it he
may be back in 2010 to vie
once again for top honours.

GLC staff and friends at the 2009
Hotdoggin' Après Party warm
up with some pre-limbo-contest
stretching. PHOTO ANDY DITTRICH

The women's event was nabbed by Meredith "I Came for One
Beer" Oatley, with a stellar dance-infused performance, followed by Cronifer "The Torch" Ingram and Melissa "Groove
Child" Leitch. In the hot-dog-eating contest, Al Quinlan was
narrowly edged out by the only canine contestant, Sammy, who
had to rely, though not without controversy, on a human assistant. I was already bent well out of shape by the time the limbo
contest started, so I opted to watch the incredible display of
grace and athleticism that kicked off the dance portion of the
party. The victor of the limbo was Bethany Parsons, and the
Best Buns in Tight Pants Contest was tightly contested between
Christie McBummerson and Julia Longbottom.

I'd say the Hotdoggin' Après Party has proven itself plenty
silly enough to grow into a time-honoured tradition.

Of Barrels and Fish

One of Whistler's oldest spring traditions involved placing a forty-five gallon drum on the south end of Alta Lake, and letting community members guess when the ice would melt and cause it to float past Cypress Point. The Ice Break Raffle began in the late fifties as a fundraiser for the Alta Lake volunteer fire department. Florence Petersen was the first-ever winner of the event, and she described to me how her friend Gerta Ples would sight a line from the frame of her kitchen window across to the opposite shore to determine when exactly the barrel floated past the watershed divide at the centre of the lake.

Some time in the early eighties, just as Whistler was becoming known as the number one ski resort in North America, the Ice Break Raffle drifted into oblivion. Twenty years later, on Easter weekend in 2002, I was sitting by my dining room window, enjoying the scene that Charlie Doyle had painted on his first day in Whistler, speculating on when the ice would melt and wondering whatever happened to the barrel raffle. Next thing I knew I'd rounded up a forty-five-gallon drum and was sliding it out to the middle of the southern end of the lake in my canoe, holding on to the gunnels so as not to break through the ice—it was already a little late in the season. The Ice Break Raffle had sprung back into existence, this time as a fundraiser for the Alta Lake School (now the Whistler Waldorf School).

The tradition has gradually re-entered the community's imagination, and this year garnered close to a thousand entries. It has also provided me with no shortage of misadventures while placing and retrieving the barrel. While I've never left the placement of the barrel as late as the Easter weekend again, I've still encountered my fair share of flimsy ice. One year with a particularly poor ice pack, I headed out too late in the season, clad in snowshoes and carrying a twenty-foot mast while rolling the barrel ahead of me. The snowshoes seemed a good idea

until one of them briefly broke through and I suddenly realized how quickly they would switch from help to hindrance if
I ended up in the water. Another year, the barrel was out nice
and early, but I hadn't yet discovered the importance of ballast
for holding it in place. There were some huge southern winds
blowing in February, and one afternoon I received a call from
my neighbour Dave Galt. "Ah, Stephen," he said. "I don't know
if you've been watching the lake, but I just saw your barrel roll
past here at about sixty miles an hour." I found it in a pile of
rocks at the north end of the lake, put it back in place and loaded it with a few rocks. The rocks or water I've since used for
ballast, however, have made the barrel extremely difficult to lift
back into the boat. Wrestling it back into the tippy canoe while
surrounded by ice floes ranks right up there among the more
stupid acts I've committed, and I've since adapted my retrieval
technique by tying a rope around the barrel plug and towing it
to shore.

This year's raffle winner was long-time local and Whistler
taxi driver "Dogger" Don Eagleton. As I handed him the Ice
Break Trophy with his name inscribed and the $250 first prize,
Dogger, who lives on the eastern shore of the lake in Alta Vista,
said, "Just before I bought my tickets I was out there chopping
through to make an ice rink and I knew it was really thick so I
gave it an extra couple of weeks." There were a dozen guesses
on the right date of April 29, including Florence Petersen's, but
Dogger's was closest to the precise time of 6:50 p.m. and ten
seconds. "It feels great," he added. "It's like flicking a dime off
your fingers and having it land on the end of a needle."

This winter the snow hardly fell in December and January,
and had it not been for the extensive snow-making now in place
on Whistler and Blackcomb, the ski operation might have had
to close for a time, as it did in 1976–77. Just like that winter,
it proved to be another great year for ice-skating on the lakes.

The snow did finally arrive in late February and March, but I ended up skating and playing hockey as many times as I skied this year. Working on this book in the middle of the day, I'd often look out my office window and see the local boys out by Blueberry Hill or Adventures West playing a game of shinny. Jim Warrin, Binty Massey, Phil Jensen, Brett Wood or any number of revolving regulars might be playing on any given day, but there's one guy whose presence you could count on: Eric Crowe. Eric is the unofficial commissioner of Alta Lake hockey. Living at the foot of Lorimer Road, he goes out to check on the ice regularly and starts shovelling a rink whenever the weather looks promising. More than that, he manages to entice assistant commissioner Steve Laing and others to join in the work until a good-sized rink is ready for use. After that it's just maintenance until the next snowstorm; and if the storm brings too much snow to shovel, well, then it's time to go skiing.

But it's not just a smooth ice surface that Eric is interested in when it comes to Alta Lake. In the summers it's what lies

When the snow is a little sparse on the mountains, games of shinny flourish on Alta Lake. PHOTO BONNY MAKAREWICZ

beneath the surface that commands his attention, most notably, the fish. As well as being a well-respected mountain bike racer, municipal parks worker, skier, father of two and husband to Michelle, Eric is Whistler's foremost fish detective. "I was really keen on fishing as a kid in Ontario," he told me over an imported beer in his kitchen one afternoon. "I always had a soft spot in my heart for the little indigenous fish in the streams, the Eastern speckled trout."

Recovering after a ski injury one spring, Eric spent a lot of time fishing in the Cheakamus River for steelhead trout. "After catch and release was introduced there were some really good runs. I was able to differentiate between different types of steelhead," he said. Eric had been reading the literature on fish species and asking questions about them since he was twelve years old. It was after another injury that those questions began to focus closer to home, at Alta Lake and the River of Golden Dreams. "I went down the River of Golden Dreams with a mask, snorkel and a wetsuit. You wouldn't see any fish at all, then all of a sudden where some small tributary streams came in there'd be fifty big rainbow trout. I started asking myself, 'Why at these creeks? Why at such an early time of the year? Were these females drawn to the vital populations of males in those backwaters?'"

This was where Eric's detective work took a decidedly scientific and controversial turn. He started reading Allan Costello's UBC doctoral thesis, *The Origin and Maintenance of Small Populations of Cutthroat Trout,* and learned that the fish has unique ways of maintaining genetic diversity in relatively small ecosystems. Some male trout reach sexual maturity as early as two years of age, and some will reside in side streams, remain small and eventually reintroduce their genetic material back to the larger population. "There are orgies, when more than one generation will mate with the females," Eric said.

What shakes Alta Lake's fishing history to its roots, however, is Eric's belief that the rainbow trout, long thought to be indigenous to the lake, were actually introduced in the early twentieth century. "Now there's all these new girls in town," he said of the rainbows. I point out the obvious parallel with the ski-bum population in the fall, but the history of the Whistler fish population is our real focus here. "At first you get hybrid vitality, but that vitality only happens for a short time while they're getting new genetic material. Soon the rainbow hybrids are spawning with hybrids," Eric said. The result, he believes, is a lake full of small rainbow trout lacking in vitality—the current situation in Alta Lake.

Eric's sleuthing uncovered a sockeye hatchery that operated from 1905 to 1935 at Owl Creek near Pemberton. Kamloops trout (the Gerard strain originally from Kootenay Lake) were also reared there and introduced into Alta Lake and probably many lakes in the area at the time. Rainbow trout, Eric says, is really just a hatchery name. He believes that the true original fish in Alta Lake were Coastal cutthroat, which maintained their genetic diversity as previously described. Johnny Jones, an archeological field technician with the Mount Currie band, has told Eric that the Lil'wat name for coastal cutthroat, sts'ets'kwaoz7ú7el, translates as "real original trout."

Despite the mounting body of evidence, Eric's theory hasn't been wholeheartedly embraced. After all, his cutthroat research pokes holes in the tidy history of a town that began with guests at Rainbow Lodge fishing for the naturally plentiful rainbow trout. Fish that are introduced from elsewhere, Eric says, will never fully thrive here for a host of reasons—they're out of sync. "What's important is to understand the species and protect it where it is. Instead of trying to do a sports fishery, it should be done with a scientific or naturalists' approach—trying to make it work in terms of ecology instead of economy.

Acknowledging the truth is our only opportunity to try to make it thrive," he said.

The burden of proof, however, still rests on Eric. Last summer he hiked up to small lakes and waterways in the surrounding mountains to get DNA samples of trout he believed were uncorrupted by introduced species. So far his efforts have turned up only rainbow DNA. But Eric believes he may have been looking in the wrong places. The small vital populations in backwaters off of the River of Golden Dreams may still turn up what he's looking for. And to complicate the fish detective's work further, there is the story of the young David Fairhurst who grew up at Cypress Lodge in the sixties. David now lives on Vancouver Island and is very knowledgeable in fisheries himself. As a young boy he loved nothing better than to hike up to the surrounding lakes and waterways with a bucket of Alta Lake trout to ensure their proliferation far and wide.

The Party Barge

It's been said that necessity is the mother of invention, and that adage certainly holds true for the genesis of the Party Barge. In the early seventies, Whistler's valley bottom was a much more natural and wetland-rich place than it is today, and part of that richness was an abundance of mosquitoes and blackflies. In the reeds at the south end of Alta Lake, their populations were particularly healthy. "The concept," recalled captain and chief pilot of the Party Barge, Roger Moxley, "was to basically put a motor on the dock, motor out into the middle and kind of float around, as the bugs were no where near as bad out there as they were around the shoreline."

At Tokum Corners, where a classic old cedar-shake cabin sat next to the railway tracks at the southwest end of the lake until it was torn down in the early nineties, photographer George Benjamin had already experimented with the Party

Barge concept. Tokum was known as a place of innovation and experimentation, turning out homebrewed Tokum Tonic beer in labelled stubbies and launching test rockets with the West Side Pyromaniacs Association run by John Heatherington and Bruce Prentice. The Party Barge Division, Roger recalled, had a little three-horsepower motor on the Tokum dock, which they putted out onto the lake maybe three times a year. Roger, who was living with his partner Ebe Lepp at Chaplinville, the site of the old Alta Lake townsite, saw the possibilities and put his six-foot-four-inch frame into constructing his own barge. "I built it all out of solid logs," he told me over his cellphone while strolling through Peachland, his current home base in the Okanagan. "The original dock, when it had good flotation, could have about twenty-five people on it before it started sinking." Over a quarter of a century later, that same dock still plies the waters of Alta Lake, holding a wealth of stories in its beer- and rain-soaked decking, Astroturf and well-weathered La-Z-Boy couches. It is now harboured out front of co-pilot Dave Galt's home at Kelso Lodge on the west side of the lake. "Dave has put some floatation, like Styrofoam and stuff underneath it," Roger said. "It's getting a little waterlogged now. We can only handle about thirteen people on it at once."

While the barge has hosted more than its fair share of parties over the years, it has also worked in the service of entertaining kids. "I did a lot of birthday parties," Roger said. "That's when I really started doing some serious barging, when our son Warren came along." Roger and Ebe provided catering services for film crews on location in the Vancouver area and sometimes farther afield. The many productions they've worked on include *First Blood* with Sylvester Stallone, *21 Jump Street* and *The X-Files*. After being constantly on the road and hiring nannies to look after Warren, it eventually made more sense for one of them to stay home. "I basically became a house husband," Roger said, "spending most of my summers taking him and a bunch of his buddies out. It's what we did for summer fun."

And then there were the cruises for so-called grown-ups. The Party Barge has hosted staff parties for Tapley's Pub, Citta', the Longhorn, the Whistler Mountain grooming crew and many others, including a stagette with about twenty naked girls who tried to talk Alfie, Roger's crew member at the time, into becoming their male stripper. It was with the grooming crew, however, that Roger ran into his first trouble with the Whistler bylaw department. "The boys brought out these massive Yamaha speakers with a little generator and we actually got four noise complaints from as far away as Alpine Meadows," Roger recalled. "That was when Calvin [Logue] was running around the lake trying to nail us down, back when bylaw didn't have a boat. When we pulled into Tokum Corners, he came running down the tracks and told us to turn it down. Well, we turned it down until he disappeared back up the cut there to the highway, and then back it cranked up again and then down the lake we went. Oh yeah. We kept him busy for a day."

The only other time Roger had the law after him on the lake was during a staff barge cruise for Tapley's Pub. "It was at the height of fire season," he said. "I had a beer keg cut in half, which we barbecued on, and then after the barbecue was over we'd usually throw a couple of logs on and that's my running lights at night." Toward the end of the night while the barge was docked near the mouth of Scotia Creek, somebody across the lake mistook the keg fire for a campfire and alerted the fire department. "All of a sudden I hear sirens. They're going up and down the West Side Road trying to figure out where this fire is, and by that point I said, 'Well, we better go into silent running here.' We put the fire out, because I suspected that might have been what they were after us for. They had trucks and the RCMP and bylaw, and they covered every public access. They were shining big spotlights across the lake trying to find us, but we kind of drifted down and right close to the shore- line. I pulled in at that time to the Ugly American's, we called a couple of cabs and we all got off board before we got in trouble.

"The next day at Tapley's, Tony Evans who was our fire chief at the time . . . comes up to me and he goes, 'I know that was you out there last night. You had a fire.' I said, 'Tony, Tony, come on. Give me a break here. I mean, I had a con- tained fire on my barge.' He says, 'Well, worst-case scenario, you could have been all so drunk, you fall off your barge, your barge drifts across the lake to Blueberry Hill—and you could have set the whole Blueberry Hill on fire and burned Whistler down.'"

Fortunately, the Party Barge has always managed to avoid worst-case scenarios. And while the open seas of Alta Lake aren't considered international waters, Roger believes that because of the size of the lake, they do fall under the federal Waterways Act rather than entirely under municipal control. "The only thing the municipality could do was enforce the speed limit to eight knots, so that's why I was able always to do what I was doing, although a lot of people thought that I was grandfathered. Quite frankly it's because I've been doing it as long as I have and I've done it without incident. I've never had one drowning and I think the worst that's ever happened was me falling down drunk and cutting my knee one time. That was about the extent of injuries on the high seas."

The heyday of the Party Barge was undoubtedly the eight straight years that it was put into service for the Dave Murray Summer Ski Camp. In the eighties, at the end of each of the two week-long adult camps, Dave Murray arranged with Roger to take his campers out on the barge for their wrap-up party. The numbers warranted stringing a number of docks together, with contributions from various neighbours along the west side of the lake including Jan and Rob Burgess and Paul Mathews. Joel Thibault, with the help of Michelle Bush (before she ran off to join the circus), catered the cruises, complete with white tablecloths, fine food and wines and a powerful stereo system. "These were people that literally came from all around the world to this camp," Roger recalled. "And there were people that actually stayed another week just so they could go out and have another barge cruise. It was actually billed as one of the highlights of the summer camp; there were people that came back year after year." Unable to be officially remunerated for his captaining services due to liability concerns, Roger was paid through a trade-off agreement. "I'd get a dual mountain [season's] pass for doing those two trips," he said. "That's how I got my pass for almost ten years."

Piloting SS *Party Barge* for the camps was no small feat. The first year, with a ten-horsepower motor, Roger was pushing about sixty feet of barge with sixty-five or seventy people and all the catering equipment aboard. "I was just doing that by the seat of my pants. If that engine had crapped out we would have been down in the weeds at Adventures West. A couple of times when the wind did come up quite drastically I had to do the zigzag back." As the camps grew in popularity, so too did the size of the Party Barge. "The biggest cruise I did, I was pushing 160 feet of float and I had

Roger Moxley plies the high seas of Alta Lake on his Party Barge with son Zachary. PHOTO COURTESY STEPHANIE REESOR

117 people out there with porta-potties, and two barges were all barbecues and just a whole unbelievable spread of food," Roger said.

The wind came up for that cruise too, but this time Roger had a bit more power behind the extended barge. His old crewmate Alfie had a connection with OMC in Ontario, and Roger came home one day to find three brand-new fifteen-horsepower Evinrude engines sitting on his deck with a note: "Here, have fun. Use them for the summer, send us some pictures, and just box them up and send them back at the end of the summer." So, with 160 feet of float and nearly 120 partiers, the cruise set sail. "I couldn't even see the front of this thing," Roger recalled. "I had a guy on the front with a walkie-talkie telling me roughly how close I'm getting so I could start [turning], with that many people and the weight. Actually, with the wind and everything, I ended up doing absolutely the most perfect landing ever. This guy comes down to me, and he goes, 'Hi, I'm Bodey.' This guy's a third-generation Mississippi riverboat pilot, and he says, 'Man, you've got the touch. I was really wondering how you were going to pull this off with so little horsepower and this mass of people and stuff.' And then months later I started getting the Mississippi Riverboat Pilots' Association newsletter every four months, and a baseball cap and a T-shirt from the association. And he says, 'Any time you want a job, just come down and look me up.'"

With his honorary credentials and the many connections made through the Dave Murray camps, interest in the Party Barge continued to grow. After a long day of cruising, Roger and his crew would often end up at either Tapley's or Umberto's, where Alfie's girlfriend worked. "We would go in there after a day of barging, and there would be people saying, 'I saw you out there. Can I hire your barge tomorrow?' and I'd say, 'Well, I don't really do that.' When they all of a sudden peel off three or four brown ones, they've got my attention. They would bring all this food and booze and everything, and we'd go out there for the typical Gilligan's three-hour cruise. Well, we wouldn't get back in until midnight or whatever."

One of Roger's repeat clients was Masayoshi Ohkubo, owner of Nippon Cable, Sun Peaks Resort and previous partial owner of Intrawest. "Every time he came to Whistler in the summer," Roger recalled, "he would bring his whole family and his entourage of these Japanese guys and they'd give me little presents and stuff. He would say he would have more fun on that barge than he did on his yacht in the Tokyo Harbour. We'd always cruise by the Whistler Lodge area where—that was still sort of the naked beach in Whistler—and the boys always got a good thrill about seeing these naked mountain girls."

Another client was a big-time Miami lawyer, Roger recalled. "He was with the summer camps. His wife had the big store-bought tits, and George was a big, overweight lawyer kind of guy, all big gold chains and everything around his neck. When he first came down he looks up at the public dock one way and down the other way, and he goes, 'You'd never be able to do this in America, you know.'"

With business so good, Roger considered trying to legitimize the barge one summer. "I went over to municipal hall and I said, 'Is there any chance you can give me a licence?' They just laughed and said, 'No, you just keep doing it the way you're doing it, because otherwise we're just going to open up a whole can of worms.'" He also phoned the Coast Guard one year when Dave Murray was wondering about liability for the summer camps. "I said, 'Listen, I'm pushing 160 feet, I've got 150 people out there, and I'm doing this little charter cruise.' And the guy, I can hear him flipping through these pages, and he goes, 'Well, you come under the same classification as BC Ferries. You've got to have on-deck fire pumps, lifeboats.' I said, 'No, no, this is just a raft moving around a small lake at about a knot-and-a-half.' And he said, 'Well, we don't really have any rules for something like that. Just carry on if you've been doing this for a while.'"

One of the less likely groups to hire out the Party Barge for an afternoon of cruising was the Howe Sound school district administration. "There was probably about forty of them," Roger recalled. "All the principals, vice-principals, all their administration. They came on board with maybe a couple of two-fours of beer and I just looked at the main guy and I said, 'Buddy, how long do you think that's going to last with a crew of thirsty people like you? Have you got a cellphone?' 'Yeah.' 'You got a credit card?' 'Yeah.' I said, 'Here, give me your phone, and by the time we get down the lake I'll have some more ciders and beers and stuff.' So I called Tapley's and they organized a cab and sure enough we had the cab drop off another six two-fours and a bunch of ciders. Everybody had just a wonderful time. All those sort of straight school marms were dropping their hair down by the end of the cruise."

For all the wild times the Party Barge has facilitated on Alta Lake, it has also occasionally played the role of search and rescue craft. When windsurfing was popular on the lake in the seventies and eighties, beginners who started at the south end at Wayside or Lakeside Park inevitably rode the 'Keg Express,' powered by the prevailing southerly winds, until they were mired in the reeds near Adventures West and the old Keg restaurant. "We used to rescue these people that were just totally exhausted and pull them out of the weeds, and we'd drag 'em back up to the public dock," Roger said.

Another rescue involved a couple of cops, one of them an undercover narcotics officer, who'd flipped their Hobie Cat near the north end of the lake. "We saw these guys having issues," Roger remembered. "They had the thing stuck upside-down, so Dave [Galt] and I go, 'Maybe we better go over there and give these people a hand.' They looked like they were in trouble because the boat was on its side and then it went right upside-down and the mast got stuck in the mud. As we got closer to the vessel, we realized who it was. I knew Russ quite well. It was, 'Oh, David, it's the boys. Let's just turn around and leave them.' And Russ goes, 'Moxley, you get back here right now or you'll get tickets until they're coming out your yingyang.' So we went over and helped them pull the mast out of the mud and sent them on their merry way."

While the early days of barging were often in the service of Roger's son Warren and his friends, it also played a role in his next relationship and the arrival of his second son, Zac. Princess Stephanie Reesor, famous for surfing the Boot Pub's pool table out of the bar and a renowned Whistler character in her own right, was down at Lakeside Park with her friend Karen Griffin the first time she saw the barge. "What is that?" she asked.

Long-time local Mike Jakobsson (seated) with friends Michelle and Kathy (standing) and dozens of others kick back for a day of cruising on Alta Lake, July 1985. In its heyday, the Party Barge carried up to 120 revellers on a flotilla of five docks for the Dave Murray Summer Ski Camp parties. PHOTO ROD HARMAN

"It's the Party Barge," Karen, a reporter and cartoonist with the *Whistler Question*, replied. "See that guy?" Princess Stephanie said, "I'm going to marry him." Thus began Whistler's own Party Barge romance.

The princess was impressed by the almost incongruous cleanliness Roger practised with the barge at the end of a day of cruising. "We had to clean the couches; he'd clean the deck. If he'd had a vacuum cleaner he would have vacuumed it." Stephanie went on plenty of barge cruises over the years, but some of her favourite moments were being out at night on the quiet lake. "I used to sleep out on it a lot. Right out in the middle of the lake when it was meteor showers. We'd start down by Wayside, and we'd go to sleep and wake up in front of Chaplinville," she said. "The lake is calm and the sun's coming up and it's so beautiful."

The barge has always been popular with the media as well. Photos have appeared in the *Province* and the *Vancouver Sun*, and it has been filmed by CBC and CTV. Other film crews have hired Roger to take them out on the water so they could get good shots of Whistler peak from the middle of the lake. The one media moment that sticks in his mind, however, was during one of the Murray camps. "CBC was there and they were doing a little thing on the barge and the summer camp. So everybody's onboard and we're just heading out, and I'm standing at the back, like [Exxon Valdez] Captain Hazelwood, tipping my first cocktail of the day, and they get this on film. It was one of those Sunday-night fillers on the CBC *National*. So Monday morning I get a call from my mother and she goes, 'I saw you on the news last night, and I see you're still smoking and drinking.' I could not believe it that she actually saw that."

You might be able to avoid the mosquitoes and blackflies out on the Party Barge, but not necessarily the watchful eye of your mother.

10

ULLR, GOD OF SKIING

The two winters prior to 1976–77 were exceptionally good snow years in Whistler. In the fall of 1974, the year Ullr Fest was born, eighteen-year-old Steve Anderson moved to Whistler from Deep Cove in North Vancouver. He and a couple of buddies rented an A-frame cabin from John Taylor at the south end of Nita Lake. The flat land next to the lake, now predominated by the Nita Lake Lodge, was then home to the 1920s-built Jordan's Lodge, a weathered log cabin called the Trap and the A-frame that had been moved there from the base of the lifts.

The young ski bums would regularly see a much older member of the tribe hike down from his trailer above Alta Lake Road and cross the bridge over Alta Creek next to their cabin, the quickest shortcut to the Gondola Barn. "We'd look out our window," Steve told me over a few cold pints at Brandy's, "and go, 'Who is this old guy going through?' You know, he must have been about forty years old. We were eighteen, [and we thought] 'This guy's ancient.' And we were always wondering, who the hell is this character?"

The elder statesman ski bum, already sporting his trademark long, flowing beard, was one Albert John Hare, known in these parts as Rabbit. He had first come to Whistler to ski with some Vancouver colleagues and after the second visit simply told them, 'I'm not going back.' Steve and his housemates eventually met John on the mountain while skiing one day and quickly became good buddies. Steve recalled the meeting, mimicking the diminutive Englishman's accent. "'So, you're the guys from that A-frame.' He was your proverbial ski bum," Steve recalled. "He worked at the clothing department at the Bay [in Vancouver], I think, for years and years. And then he got into snow skiing, and just went, 'Wait a minute, this is what I want to do.' And he did it every single day he could. He was up there, didn't matter what the weather was."

Early in the winter of 1974, the young ski bums on the shore of Nita Lake got it into their heads to perform a sacrificial ski

Albert John "Rabbit" Hare shows proper technique in the "No Biking" area outside the village liquor store. PHOTO COURTESY *WHISTLER ANSWER*

offering to Ullr, the god of skiing. Steve's friend Tony Kirkwood, who started the renegade Fitzsimmons Ski School on Whistler Mountain, had a friend named Marco Pfeiffer living with him. "Marco was a reforming heroin addict from the West End of Vancouver, where Kirkwood's from," Steve recalled. "He was on the junk and he came up here to clean out. We got him hooked on sports and off of the heroin. Gave him something else to get high on. It worked. He never went back to the heroin.

"He had the little pin that said "Ullr," and he was like, 'Fucking god of snow, man. This is the god of snow.' He was a strange son of a bitch. And he said, 'We've got to do a sacrifice for more snow.'" With the idea heartily embraced by all, they made preparations for the event. The site they chose was on the ice in front of Jordan's Lodge, directly across the lake from Tyrol Lodge. Calona Wines still sold wine in gallon jugs back then, which the worshippers fortified with plenty of vitamins to enhance the religious aspect of the ritual. "It was just a madcap, crazed affair, dancing around the fire in the middle of the

Ullr, Norse god of skiing, reigns supreme in the Coast Mountains. PHOTO & SCULPTURE MUSHROOM MARK

lake," Steve said. "Rabbit was part of the first ski burn we had, the first sacrifice to Ullr. Oh yeah, Rabbit was in on that deal. He just went, 'These are the kind of guys I want to hang out with. They're really, really twisted people.' I still remember that first ski-burning, it was mental. Everybody dancing around in circles, hooting and hollering."

Lo and behold, the snow fell in droves that winter, and thus an annual ritual was born. As with any religion, the proper observances quickly took form. "There were rules, you know," Steve said. "Like, you can't burn shit, it's got to be good skis." The effigy was another key element in the Ullr sacrifice. "We would always pick a prominent figure in town and make an effigy out of them, stuff the ski clothes with paper and gasoline." Apt comparisons to Robin Hardy's cult horror film *The Wicker Man* spring to mind. It was clear to the worshippers that individuals in positions of power sometimes stray from the path of truth, and in Whistler money was often the deity of choice. The young ski bums knew that from the perspective of the gods, a thin line indeed separates the powerbroker from the fool.

Shawn Walsh traditionally lit the effigy by shooting a flaming arrow from a bow. His execution was completely in keeping with depictions of the old Norse god. Known in Norse mythology as the ski god, bow god, hunting god and shield god, Ullr also carried a shield that was called his ship, and probably referred to his skis. In the *Prose Edda*, a book of Norse lore by thirteenth-century Icelandic poet Snorri Sturlusun, Ullr, son of Sif and stepson of Thor, is described as "such a good archer and ski runner that no one can rival him." I'm pretty certain that Marco Pfeiffer and his pals were unaware that Ullr in Old Norse means "glory" or "glorious one," and that a related inscription found on a piece of a scabbard from 200 AD means "servant of the glorious one," but the latter term could certainly have described the wine-and-drug-frenzied ski bums on Nita Lake in 1974.

Meanwhile, up on the mountain the skiing was exceptional and the festivities continued. While the Ullr burn was strictly an annual event, smaller fires were kept kindled atop the mountain in the forest or downstairs in the Roundhouse throughout the winter. It was likely these early days of research that led to Rabbit's most famous and much-quoted saying: "Leave no turn unstoned." After a good day of "fresh air" and exercise on the mountain, the partying continued in the valley. "The partying was pretty legendary with Rabbit," Steve said, "right back to where The Keg used to be. The mosh pits out back around the fire pit, and crazy antics going on, and then the next thing his pants are down at his ankles. He was famous for taking his clothes off. He was always doing that."

The Ullr sacrifices also continued in the valley, and they began to gather many new initiates. "Our religion," Steve said with a laugh. "Well, we weren't very God-fearing people. What was Rabbit's favourite saying? I think he ripped it off from Keith Richards: 'I love God, but I hate preachers.'" As is true among many mountain cultures, the ski bums had a healthy appreciation for irreverence, especially when it came to the Ullr burn.

"It went to different venues," Steve recalled. "I remember we did a couple where the village is now, a big parking lot. We had a giant bonfire going, the skis, effigies, everything. We had little Volkswagen cars doing doughnuts in the parking lot. People were just coming in off the road going, 'What the hell is going on?! Whaa, this is great.' That one turned into a big party. That was huge."

One year the Ullr Fest was held at a house on Wedgeview Drive that Steve rented with Vincent "Binty" Massey, who still has a pottery studio just down the road. "We decided to have one

To the horror of its early disciples, Ullr Fest was adopted by Whistler Mountain in the 1980s. Note the lack of an effigy. PHOTO BRIAN HYDESMITH

up there in Alpine Meadows. That's the year we almost burned down the house. The cedar Pan-Abode was getting pretty hot, and we were getting freaked out. I remember we were all still inside, loading up, as it was referred to, before heading outside. We looked out the window, and somebody had lit the effigy before any of us." The house survived the night, but the incident was perhaps the first sign of a religion moving out of the hands of its original disciples and beginning to stray from its prescribed rituals.

Some years Ullr seemed more willing to bestow his gifts if the sacrifice included some particularly valuable ski equipment. One of the disciples had picked a new pair of skis from the racks at the base of the gondola. The skis had just been out on their first day with their owner, a prominent mountain ski director who had made several appearances as an effigy atop Ullr's offerings. The guys were all duly impressed, but with the authorities out looking high and low for the skis, "they" were way too hot to ski on," Steve said. Then the idea emerged, as if planted by the gods themselves: "Burn 'em! We'll have to burn 'em!" And so it was. A brand new pair of Dynastar S730s mounted with the latest Solomon 555 Golds went up in a spectacular flaming offer to the Glorious One. "That was a very good season," Steve pointed out. "That was a giant snow year."

It may be hard to imagine, but the ski bums eventually began to grow up just a little. Steve met Susi Wurm, now his wife and mother to their daughter Marli, who had stayed at the Tyrol Lodge with her family in the seventies and perhaps witnessed the early Ullr fires across the lake from the lodge balcony. Rabbit also met his future wife, Janice "Rocky" Runnalls, and started a family. Settling down for the couple did not involve a house in the burbs and a nine-to-five job. They moved to the top of Whistler Mountain where they were hired to caretake the alpine office building.

Rocky and Rabbit's first daughter, Jessica "Pika" Hare, remembers living at the top of the mountain. "Some of my strongest memories," she told me, "are of being up there in the summer with no one around. You used to be able to go up on top of the building. I remember having a bath and all of us going up there, and the moon's out and the sky is clear. And just walking around in the summer over to Harmony and the little lakes."

The only neighbours were the Whistler marmots that sunned themselves on the rocks, and the little rock rabbits that were Jessica's namesakes, darting among the dwarfed trees. In the winter, the Hares' mountaintop lair proved a great stopping-in place for ski-bum friends. "That turned out to be quite a hangout. It was like our lunchroom," Steve said. After five years at the top of the world, Jessica's sister Tara was born in 1984, and the Hares moved to midstation to caretake another building and start the lifts in the mornings. "I'd ski down to school with my dad," Jessica said. "He would take my skis and boots, and I'd take the bus to Creekside after school and ride back up the gondola. Sometimes we did it by bike in the summer." Steve Anderson recalled the socializing at the midstation house. "I remember he would start up the gondola and we would all pile down there, Shawn Walsh and myself and Herbie and the girls. Rabbit would start up the lift and we'd all pile in and go up there for dinner. It was like a personal lift. My favourite night was a Sunday night because you'd get up there and you'd walk out onto the top of Insanity and watch the snake, the line of red tail lights all heading south down the road, the red snake."

Life on the mountain ended with an unfortunate incident in 1986 when Laura Kinney, the new caretaker in the alpine with her husband, Dave, was forced to jump from the stalled Red Chair, and with substantial injuries crawl to the bottom of the Little Red Chair to phone for help. Rabbit's position at midstation meant that he had to shoulder the brunt of responsibility in the incident and the task of firing him fell to my dad. The Hares moved to Pemberton for a couple of years, and with their third child, Dylan, on the way, Rabbit got a job with Dave Kirk at the Sportstop selling retail and eventually fitting ski boots. "I hired John because I wanted a local person to do boot-fitting," Dave told me. "And I always enjoyed some uniqueness in people and John certainly brought uniqueness. People tended to think of John as a party guy, but there was more to him than that." His work in the haberdashery department at the Bay left him with good skills for selling ski clothes, Dave said. "He could tell people whether their pants were going to fit. He knew his stuff." Rabbit also became a boot-fitting specialist, though here his knowledge didn't always lead to a harmonious relationship with the clients." His advice wasn't always accepted by the customer in the way John delivered it," Dave recalled of Rabbit's tendency to not suffer fools gladly. "As the years went by he got crustier and crustier with people." To get away from the boot-fitting bench, Rabbit finally switched to ski-tuning and rentals, and in summers worked his way up as a bike mechanic until he was managing the Bikestop. After two years of living in Pemberton, Rocky had moved to Burnaby with the kids. "My dad would come and visit us," Jessica said. "My parents were always on good terms. And we would come up a lot [to Whistler]."

Being a ski bum in your twenties is one thing, but continuing that passion through an entire life requires a whole other level of commitment. Rabbit continued to put in over a hundred days of skiing a year, sporting his new, Rossignol-sponsored fat skis. And from the moment the snow melted in the valley to the time it got too thick to ride on, he could be seen daily around town on his hybrid BMX mountain bike. With his long white hair and beard he had become a highly recognizable icon in town. When a *Vancouver Sun* photographer tried to halt proceedings on a busy summer day at the Bikestop to capture him on film, Rabbit told him in no uncertain terms, "I'm busy with a customer," earning him the *Whistler Answer's* 1993 Media Iconoclast of the Year award. For staff parties, Dave recalled, Rabbit loved to get all slicked up and dress in a fine suit and tie, harkening back to his haberdashery days. He'd arrive already well into his cups, and then continue to party with the rest of the staff. "Sometimes he'd disappear later in the evening and we'd go back to the shop and find him totally laid out on his boot-fitting bench," Dave recalled.

Rabbit's anti-establishment streak and his ability to party never left him. "He also had a pretty damn good little trapline in town here, like for booze," Steve Anderson said. "He'd go to Citta' and they'd give him a round, and then he would go to the Dubh Linn Gate, they'd give him ten rounds or whatever. The Amsterdam, that was a stop on the trapline, and he would just sort of prowl from place to place." I'd often see Rabbit at the Boot in those days too, especially when he lived just across the street at the Dirt Bag Hotel. He'd be the first one up on the dance floor, whether by himself or with whichever pretty young thing in the bar would join him, and he'd start dancing with a big smile on his face. "He'd start motoring, just fricking go and go," Steve recalled. "He was like a machine. I do remember one time at Buffalo Bills, where he got angry at the DJ, he was yelling at him, 'Play some faacking mu-sic.'" Steve mimicked Rabbit's English accent. "They were like, 'If you don't settle down we're going to throw you out of here.' He was like, 'Well, play some faacking mu-sic.' They had some big horns on the wall, like antlers of some kind. He fucking stripped them off the wall and went and attacked the DJ with these moose horns or some damn thing. [Buffalo Bills] wasn't on the trapline after that. He wasn't allowed in there anymore." At least until the bar hired a new manager.

Shortly after Rabbit turned sixty-five and retired from working summers, he was diagnosed with throat cancer. The first round of treatments went well and he was soon back in the mountains skiing and biking. I got to know Rabbit a little better during this period and we had a few good patio sessions at the Amsterdam Pub where he shared some of his practical philosophy with me: "I'm practising how to do as little as possible to a high degree of perfection," he said, "watching the grass grow and the snow melt." And: "In a small community like this, even your enemies become your friends eventually." Rabbit was referring to the fact that despite the differences he and my dad had while working on the mountain, they'd ended up on good terms.

Rabbit's second round of cancer treatment included chemotherapy and left him for a time without his trademark long white hair and beard. Since the mid-nineties he'd been renting a little out-cabin in the yard from Jim and Suzanne Watts. "He called it the 'Cottage in the Pines,'" Jim said. "And he told me the day he moved in that he wasn't going to leave until the day that he died. I asked him if that was a promise or a threat." Completely healthy at the time, his pronouncement proved prescient. The cabin was small and Rabbit used the yard as an extended living room, Jim said. Neighbours Karen and Dave Kay recalled him sitting outside during his recovery phase, slowly following the sun into their yard. Karen got her camera one afternoon to capture a shot of him resplendent under the sun in a purple robe and pillbox cap. "Right when I clicked the shutter," she told me with a laugh, "he jumped up and flashed open the robe." Rabbit hadn't lost his penchant for getting naked.

In the winter of 2000, Rabbit skied his final ski season. The cancer had moved into his lungs and he made a conscious decision not to take any more chemotherapy treatments. Friends and family helped him through, and as he'd promised, he remained in the Cottage in the Pines, to the end. "He didn't want to go to the hospital," Jessica said. "He refused. We're so lucky to have the clinic." Jessica came back from travelling and together with a close community of friends including Nina Louis, Keenan Moses, Marybeth Callaghan, Jim and Suzanne Watts, Angela Mellor and Stephanie Reesor, helped to make Rabbit's last months as comfortable as possible.

Jessica related one memorable day, less than two weeks before Rabbit passed away. "I was there in the afternoon, he was not doing well, and I needed to go off and do something. Steph Reesor came by and she couldn't stay either, so Roger [Moxley, Stephanie's partner] came by," Jessica said. "I got home and they were on their way to the Boot. They'd had some rum and Coke and whatever else, and he was fine all of a sudden. They carried him into the Boot and he sat at the bar and people bought drinks for him."

On the night that Rabbit passed away, Jessica was asleep at

home and Marybeth went over to get her. "We went there and hung out," Jessica said. "Just before he passed away they said he was looking at the pictures [of his family] on the wall. We kind of all just sat around, and we each had our moments to say 'bye.'" There was no sense in calling anyone in the middle of the night, so they had one last celebration with Rabbit. "We drank the rest of his Scotch and smoked his weed. We were sitting there listening to the Doors," Jessica said. "I took some photos and then I left before the doctor came."

Shortly after Rabbit's wake at Merlin's Pub, Nina hosted a waxing party for anybody who wanted to come by. "We waxed our skis with his ashes," Jessica said. "He used to like to go to Juniper Beach on Blackcomb and sit up there in the spring sun. There were lots of us there." With their freshly waxed boards, friends and family paid one last tribute to a true ski bum's love of the sport. Up on Whistler Mountain, Jessica did one last ceremony of her own. "I tossed some ashes behind the Roundhouse and did a few turns through them," she said.

Jessica wrote an obituary that was passed around at her dad's memorial. It read in part: "He lived life on his own terms and has hopefully instilled at least a bit of that in all of us. He would want us to ski a lot more, laugh a lot more and of course have another beer. He's well known for his ability to ski all day, party all night yet still get up and do it all over again and again and again and again."

"Leave No Turn Unstoned."

And whatever happened to the original Ullr Fest? "I think it must have gone on for about . . . ten seasons, yeah, at least," Steve said as we launched into our third or fourth pint at Brandy's. "Then the Mountain started doing it, and I remember talking with the boys about that, going 'Hey, this is really bad, they don't know what they're messing with.' They're going to have a fucking shitty snow year if they keep going the way they're going.' And they did. I think it was '83 or '84. It was just a crap snow season. Hey, let me tell you, you don't mess with the gods. I remember we referred to them as 'unsanctioned burns.'"

Some of the first Ullr Fests conducted by Whistler Mountain and later Whistler Blackcomb were huge, wild affairs. New employees living in staff housing were bused over to Dusty's to join the rest of the raging locals in a ski burning frenzy. Yet despite all the reckless abandon, the snow just didn't fall as heavily as it should have. Could it have been that the rituals weren't followed as set out by the early disciples? Who, for example, was shooting the flaming arrow into the pyre? Where was the effigy of a prominent person in town? Authority figures and bean-counters were not meant to be running the thing; their likenesses were meant to be sitting atop the flames. Perhaps Ullr wanted offerings from only the truly passionate and devoted and skiing was never really meant to thrive in a corporatized environment. That's why people left behind jobs at the Bay, or abandoned the rural fields being transformed into shopping malls, and moved to the mountains in the first place. In the new scheme of things good skis are no longer being sacrificed to Ullr; in fact, the ritual fire barely includes skis at all. Along with a free hot chocolate, little wooden ski replicas are offered to the "worshippers" to throw onto the propane-fuelled fire so that no harmful gasses are released into the atmosphere. I can almost hear the Glorious One chuckling to himself and cooking up plans with his old nemesis El Niño. Where can you find a good pair of Dynastar 5730s when you need them? Steve doesn't take kindly to what he calls the "misconceptions and false history" of the ski burns. "I've heard a lot of bullshit about the ski sacrifices over the years," he said. "Like, oh, it originated from Quebec. I'm going, 'Fuck you. It did not come from

The late Rob "Bino" Denham was one of Whistler's most dedicated ski bums. Here he explores the possibilities of melding summer and winter sports. PHOTO COURTESY WHISTLER ANSWER

Quebec, that's bullshit.' It came from Marco Pfeiffer, the Ullr pin. It's all gotten commercialized now. I mean, we're gonna have to go back full circle. It was like the counterculture, you know, I'm not sure where it is anymore."

Has Whistler been co-opted by the powers that be into the Hudson's Bay or Walmart of the mountains? Have its denizens lost their passion for irreverence, their innate ability to generate outrageous mountain tales? Hell no! I put my faith in the younger generations of Whistlerites, the ones who've been brought up on a diet of healthy disrespect for the mainstream and know the true value of life in these mountains. They tend to have a rootedness and a knowing glint in their eyes that suggests they've heard perhaps one too many twisted tales from their parents. Sure, the place is too expensive and often difficult to survive in on your own terms, but the resourceful ones will still find a way. And they'll continue to be joined by a new crop of young enthusiasts who arrive every fall from all over the world to pursue the ski-bum dream just as their parents' generation did.

There's a kind of cultural through-line that can be traced in this valley, and it shows plenty of positive signs. There may no longer be squatters' cabins next to Fitzsimmons Creek, but look at the skate park that sprang up there in the nineties through the ingenuity and volunteer efforts of Whistler's young people. It's got a similar groove and sense of community to the old squatters' village, existing on the fringe of the commercial core, a hidden gem next to the river, completely free. And look at the number of creative souls emerging from this valley: artists and musicians and scientists and writers and filmmakers and, yes, even ski bums. Whistlerites young and old are in the process of creating not just a counterculture or a mountain culture or a ski-bum culture, but a culture, period. No, I don't think the gods have forsaken us yet. If we stay true to our roots and remember what brought us here in the first place, Ullr and his cohorts on high will likely continue to shine their light and drop their bountiful snowfalls.

Before we finished our session at Brandy's, Steve recalled one last anecdote about the early Ullr Fests. "We missed one year," he said. "No burn, we didn't get it together, and that was the worst season ever, 1976–77. It was just ice-skating."

"I remember it well," I told him. "I was just a kid."